Soft Front Strong Back

A Philosophy for Business and Life

The Budo Classics N. 4

Soft Front Strong Back - A Philosophy for Business and Life

Steve Rowe

Copyright © 2023 The Ran Network

First Edition

Publisher: The Ran Network
info@therannetwork.com
https://therannetwork.com

Front cover photo: © Steve Rowe

Cover and layout design: Simone Chierchini

Some of the images utilized in this book were found online. Despite our best efforts, we could not locate the correct copyright holder. No challenge to copyright is intended

No part of this book can be reproduced or used in any form or by any means without prior written permission of the publisher

ISBN: 9798850901721

Imprint: Independently published on Amazon KDP

Steve Rowe

Soft Front Strong Back

A Philosophy for Business and Life

The Ran Network

Table of Contents

Foreword by Will Henshaw   11
Preface by Bryan Andrews   14
Introduction   16
Chapter 1 - Road to Discovery   21
Chapter 2 - The Shaolin Temple   25
Chapter 3 - Mindfulness   33
Chapter 4 - The Martial Arts   41
Chapter 5 - What the Prophets Knew   47
Chapter 6 - Suffering   57
Chapter 7 - Dealing with Violence   69
Chapter 8 - The Learning Process   73
Chapter 9 – The Dojo   83
Chapter 10 - The Business   91
Chapter 11 - Students and Teaching   103
Chapter 12 - The Future   115

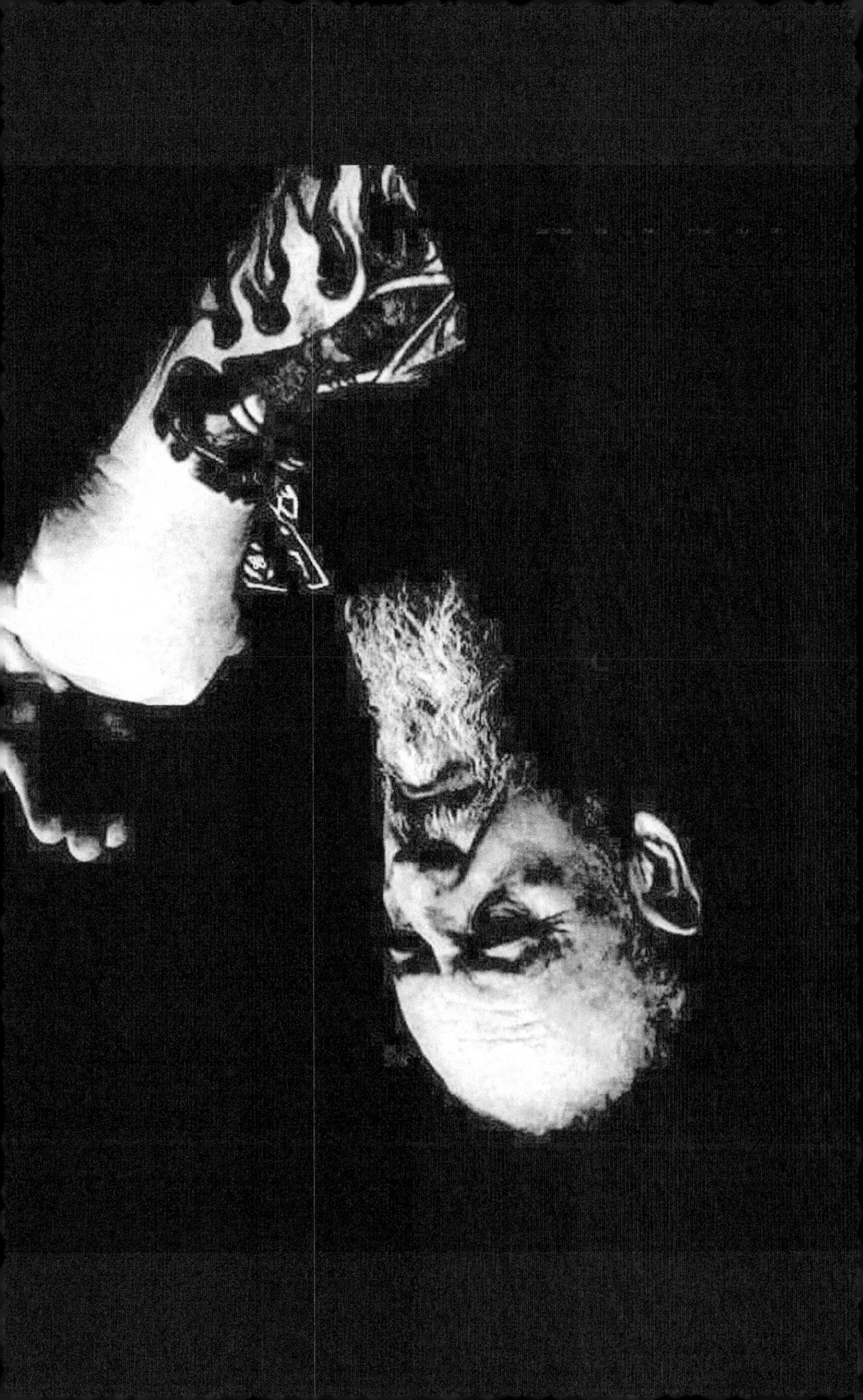

Steve Rowe is a 73yr old 9th Dan black belt in martial arts with over 50 years study in the Arts, along with meditation, mindfulness, Taoism and Buddhism. He has lived a full life with his fair share of suffering and tragedy, after having been at death's door three times with sepsis, receiving twenty-five surgeries, having a leg amputated and battling cancer. For many years he has taught worldwide the philosophies presented in this book, including to law enforcement and security professionals. He has a full time HQ in Chatham, Kent and runs a successful business with an association of thousands of followers.

I dedicate this book to all those that helped me along the way. Particularly to my family, my wife Ann, my daughter Caroline, granddaughter Rhianna and son in law Mikey. My instructors, Toru Takamizawa, Okimitsu Fuji, Jim Uglow, Ma Lee Yang and Vic Cook. My friends and students that I couldn't teach without, Martin Gatter and Ruth Dathorne, the Musil family in the Czech Republic, Ondra, Robert and Tereza and many long term students, too many to mention over the years.

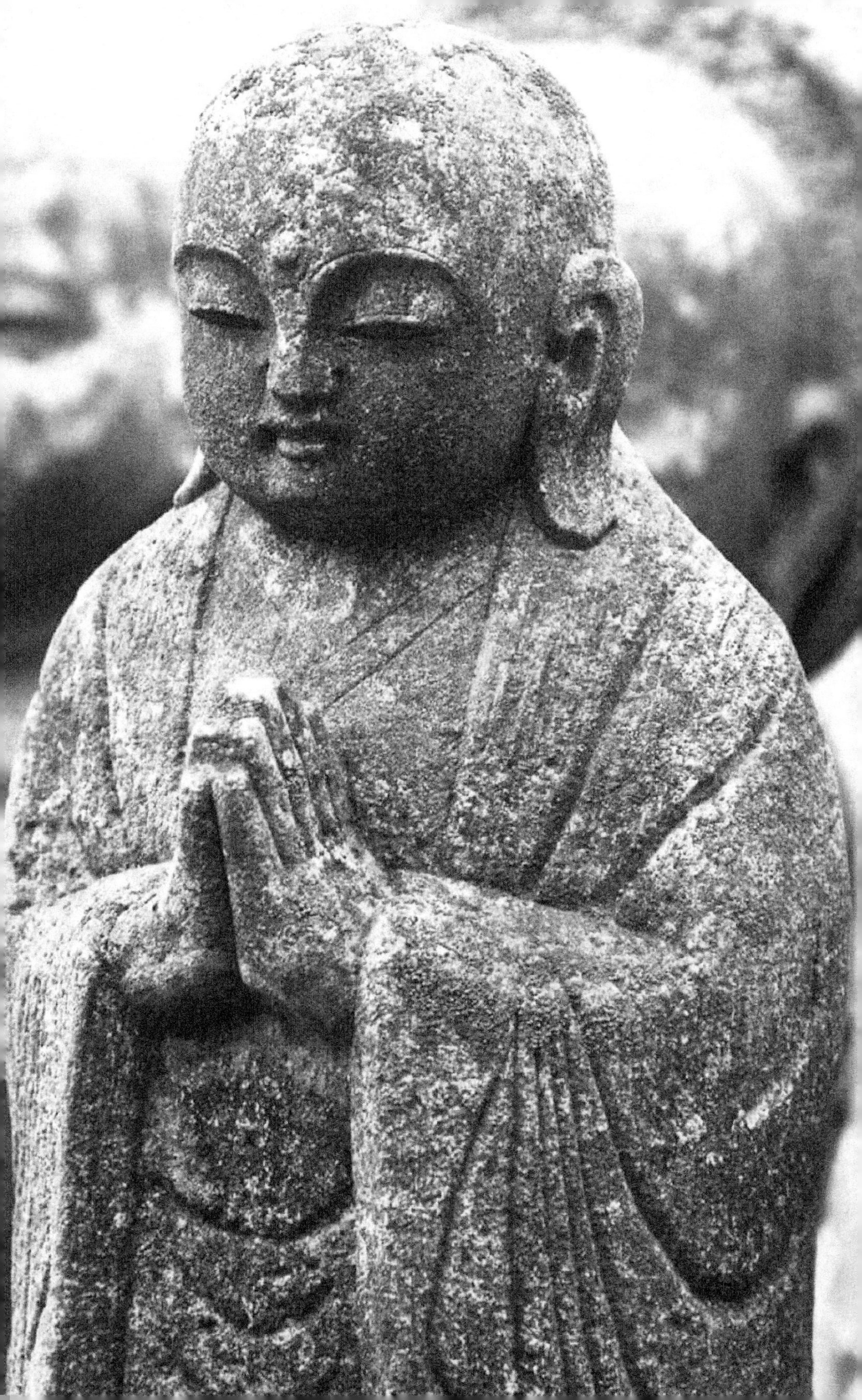

© Loki Photography

Foreword

I first met Steve Rowe in 2005, I had just completed my TV series *Mind, Body & Kick Ass Moves* for the BBC. Prior to filming I had met a lot of outstanding martial artists in 15 years of martial arts training and a lot more during the making of it. I'd also met and worked with others who were awful. Against this diverse background, Steve Rowe stood out for many reasons: yes, he had senior dan levels, had trained with some of the finest teachers and was well respected by anyone worth respecting.

We met in his dojo in Chatham, Kent, UK. After introductory pleasantries, I watched mesmerised as he transformed from the conversational gruff South Londoner into the utterly focused martial essence of the Yang family Tai Chi form.

It wasn't a performance for me or anyone: it was just him as the pure form. I was transfixed, watching a 50-something bloke fill space around him with coiled, impassive, ruthless, animal vigour and what can only be described as beautiful movement.

He offered to teach me, possibly due to my dropped jaw, or more likely because he generously teaches anyone who is keen. For me it was an obvious yes please, a unique opportunity to step inside that level of skill, and to get to know the person who had mastered it, and hopefully try to emulate it in any way possible.

Soft Front Strong Back

From that moment I began a journey to learn the basics, how to stand, to move, to breathe as a unified whole.

Sure I'd learnt similarish concepts in previous arts but had been a poor student and had acquired many stumbling blocks and mistakes that hampered any technique.

From weekly private lessons that removed the 'hiding at the back hoping to get it right syndrome' to the larger, open seminars, Steve Rowe has a unique and direct way to teach everything from the physicality, the form, to the feelings, sensations and philosophies behind the art. He has a very broad take on training, and was never afraid of discussing the esoteric and the arcane, having looked into most alleys in the martial maze sufficiently to have a well founded opinion.

Those basics were taught, and taught, again and again: in doing so they revealed ever more layers of advanced insight into how to express the form or move. Never daunted by my lack of skill, Steve found endless ways to teach the next truth bomb. And he didn't stop teaching ever finer polishes to those advanced basics and then honing them. Every private lesson was a light-bulb moment that changed everything in a profoundly good way. Beyond all that he became a good friend.

It is Steve's ability to see the wood for the trees, to be frank about what you were not doing right, how to correct it in any number of different and engaging ways and not get bored. He was successful at improving everyone, young, old, bouncers, special forces and old school, traditional martial artists.

This book encapsulates a lifetime of knowledge: read it, reread it, and read it again. You will be rewarded.

Will Henshaw
Producer of BBC's Mind, Body & Kickass Moves
Founder of World Of Martial Arts TV

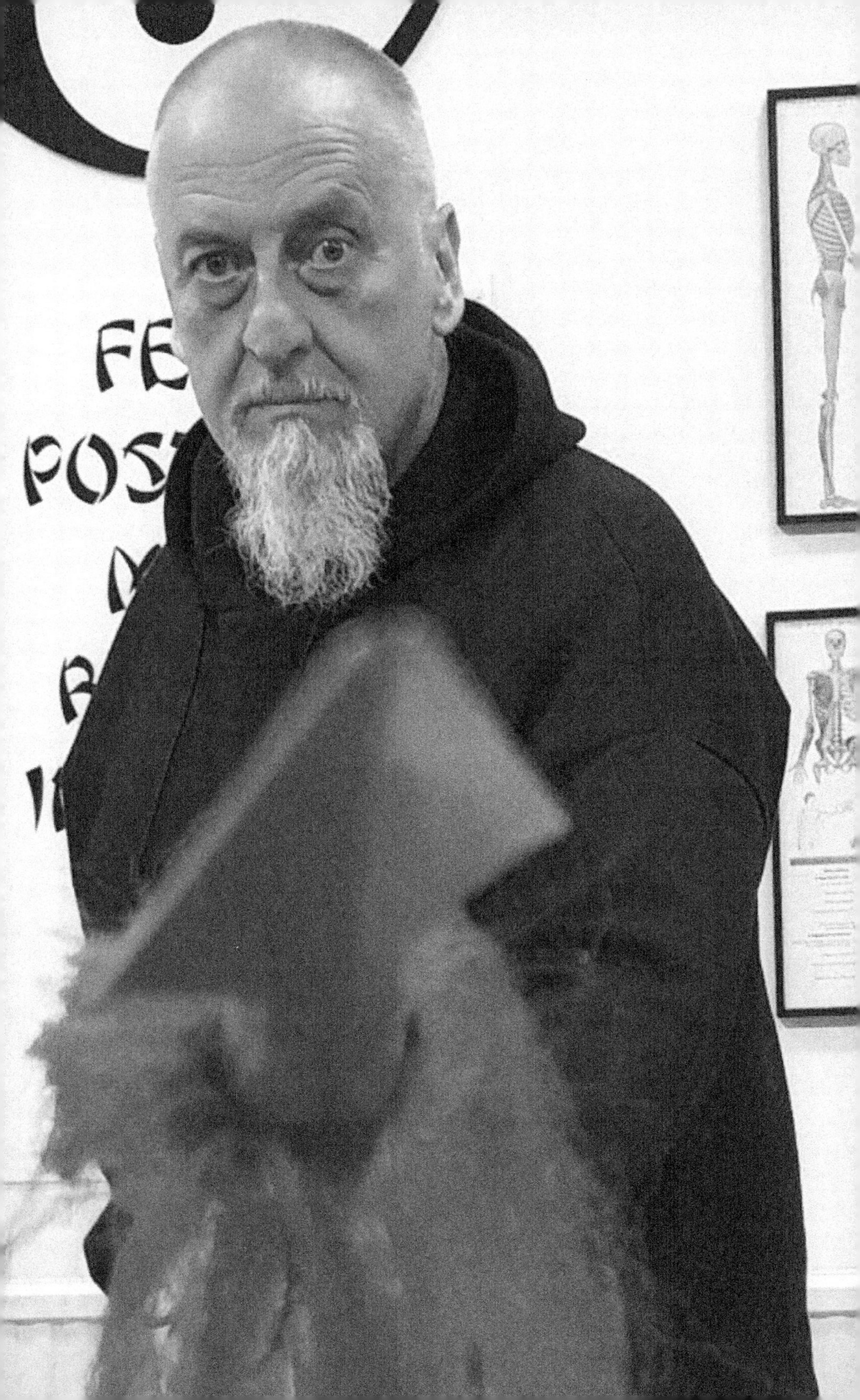

Preface

I've known of Steve Rowe for over 40 years through the influence his columns and articles across a variety of martial arts magazines had on my training. I've known Steve Rowe personally for 33 years as a teacher, a fellow martial artist and along with his whole family as friends. Steve has taught me a lot over the years in terms of martial arts business and when I've needed personal advice or support he has not hesitated to offer his wisdom. It's fair to say that I wouldn't have developed into the martial artist that I am and run the successful martial arts club that I direct without his unwavering support.

Steve has never feared to be outspoken or to tell you his mind, in fact it's one of his most enduring qualities. First and foremost, he is and always has been and always will be a martial artist with all that entails as a follower of 'The Way.' As a martial arts teacher he can be at times uplifting and also incredibly frustrating.

He won't accept substandard martial arts or the practise of martial arts which is below your best. I've watched him turn someone away from training on a seminar who had driven for over three hours to get there, because he hadn't practiced the skills from the previous seminar, so would have slowed everyone else down.

I've watched and listened to him mentoring other teachers, without any payment, to become better as both martial artists and as teachers of the martial arts. I asked him once, a long time ago, why he did it and he replied: "Because it's my responsibility and duty as a teacher of the Way".

He has the knack of being able to elicit from the practitioner a deeper understanding of their own martial art. Over many years I've watched him do this with practitioners from diverse martial arts such as Silat, Krav Maga, many different styles of Karate, Kickboxing, Kung Fu, Wing Chun and Tai Chi. His appeal is often to the 20, 30 or 40 year practitioner looking for a deeper understanding of both their own martial art and the martial arts in general.

I mentioned that I found and still find Steve to be extremely uplifting and equally as frustrating. From my own personal experience with over 25 years of private lessons with Steve, I have found that when I'm starting to feel pleased with my progress and feel like I'm starting to understand a new skill, he proceeds to unpeel another layer of the onion, at which stage I go back to the beginning again and start learning afresh. This has been an ongoing personal lesson for me, to accept the new depths of skills without getting frustrated that I can't do something yet.

In this book Steve talks about authenticity in marketing your club and being true to yourself. For many years Steve's club in Chatham has been a leading light in showing to other clubs what a good martial arts club looks like and how it should be run. Over the years Steve's role in the club has changed, with his daughter Caroline and son-in-law Mike now operationally running the club but still adhering to those principles and guidelines that for so many years Steve has espoused.

Time and again Steve shows that you don't need to be a snake oil salesman to run a high-quality and ethical martial arts club. Steve's teaching on his monthly Tai Chi coaching courses is designed to bring out the best in the students lucky enough to be training on the coaching course and learning from one of the few martial arts Masters still teaching in the UK.

Steve has a rare quality as a martial artist: he can walk the walk when it comes to martial arts, yet he's also a philosopher, a scholar and now once again an author. Some of the most fascinating and insightful times I've spent with Steve Rowe have been where we've talked about martial arts and life in general. Reading this book will give you a tiny amount of background concerning Steve's thoughts and his philosophy. No book could possibly do justice to the depth of his thinking concerning martial arts, nor the time he spends researching or testing his views. I can recommend reading his blog for more information and even better spend time with the man himself on one of his courses, I guarantee you won't be disappointed.

I'll leave with one of Steve's sayings "Often skill is not DOING something, it's NOT doing something.

Bryan Andrews
Chairman of the British Council for Chinese Martial Arts
Masters Degree in Advanced Sports (Martial Arts) Coaching Practice
6th Dan Karate

Introduction

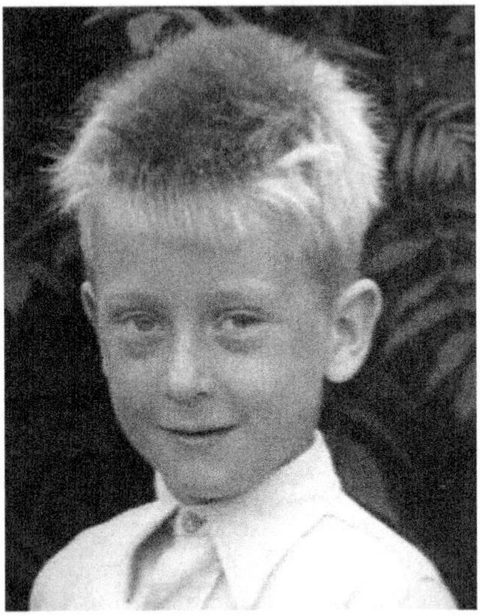

Why write this book? I tend to refer to my book writing friends as 'academics' and to myself as a 'red top newspaper columnist with tits on', meaning that I write for the masses, not the academics. The books I've written in the past are either what a publisher asked and paid me to do, small instructional booklets for students, or poetry. Because of my philosophy expressed in magazine articles, blogs and posts I've often been asked why I haven't written one on my philosophy, or in depth on my martial arts. My answer has usually been that I like to express it in short bursts so I do blogs and social media, but I now feel it's time to record it with context from my life. Why a soft front and a strong back? It encapsulates my entire philosophy. Fifty years of study have taught me that both, in balance, are necessary for a successful and happy life and business. To give a little context I was born in 1950 and spent my youth growing up on council estates with little education and no exams. I didn't get on with my family, mixed with all the wrong people, left home as soon as possible and was

Steve is in the back row, second from right (1969)

considered to be an ill educated and troubled youth.

After many low paid jobs, in 1969 I joined the London Fire Brigade but left after 3 years as I found the discipline too difficult. I became fully self employed, running a shop that I'd bought that had previously been my 'part time' work when not on shift. I caught really bad food poisoning and had to close the shop and the only work I could get was in the security trade. Over the next 12 years I worked doing all manner of security for Group 4, AFA, Chubb, EMI, Sentinel, F.W. Woolworth and Prudential Insurance, I managed cash in transit, factory guards, covertly carrying valuables and company security, I did security for nightclubs, managed store detectives, computer suite security, security for pop concerts, golf tournaments, control rooms, power stations. I also set up the first private Fire and Rescue Squad for the building of Grain Power Station, managed guard dog security including bomb searching, training security personnel in arrest restraint and personal searching, ending up as the Operations Manager for around five hundred staff. I also gave security work to quite a few martial artists over the years.

Having become a black belt in Karate in the 1970s, in 1983 I left to become a professional martial artist and because of my background, over the next 30 years I taught European presidential bodyguards, special services and law enforcement officers. I also taught doorman, security operatives, nurses, doctors, milkmen, football pools collectors, rape crisis groups, insurance agents, the staff of hundreds of different companies, people locked in prison, teachers and council workers. So I can honestly say that over that time I covered all the bases. I rarely teach security personnel now other than with the few people that I am still very close to, but it does show what's out there if you want to learn your trade properly.

1973 my first club in Greenwich, I'm front right with my two Sensei Jim Fewins and Dick Clark at the back.

As a professional martial arts teacher I realised that the mental and emotional aspects that I needed were not being addressed, so I began studying under world leading teachers in Karate, Tai Chi, Iaido and many other arts and related philosophies like Buddhism and Taoism. I also studied our western philosophies like Reiki, Wicca, Paganism, Spiritualism and anything else to do with 'internal work'. I eventually formed my own international association in 1988 and now operate a full time centre in Chatham, Kent, in the UK.

The practice of mindfulness, meditation, neigong (inner work) and qigong (energy work) calmed my body, emotions and mind allowing me to access insight and wisdom. Out of interest, I took an IQ test to discover that I had a high score putting me in the top 1%, showing that I was in fact highly intelligent and our education system couldn't cope with me.

Kicking in the 80's

I have lived a full life with my fair share of suffering and tragedy, after having been at death's door three times with sepsis, receiving twenty-five surgeries, having a leg amputated and battling cancer.

At 73 years of age I still teach seminars every weekend from a wheelchair, showing that age and disability do not preclude me from dispensing skill, insight and wisdom.

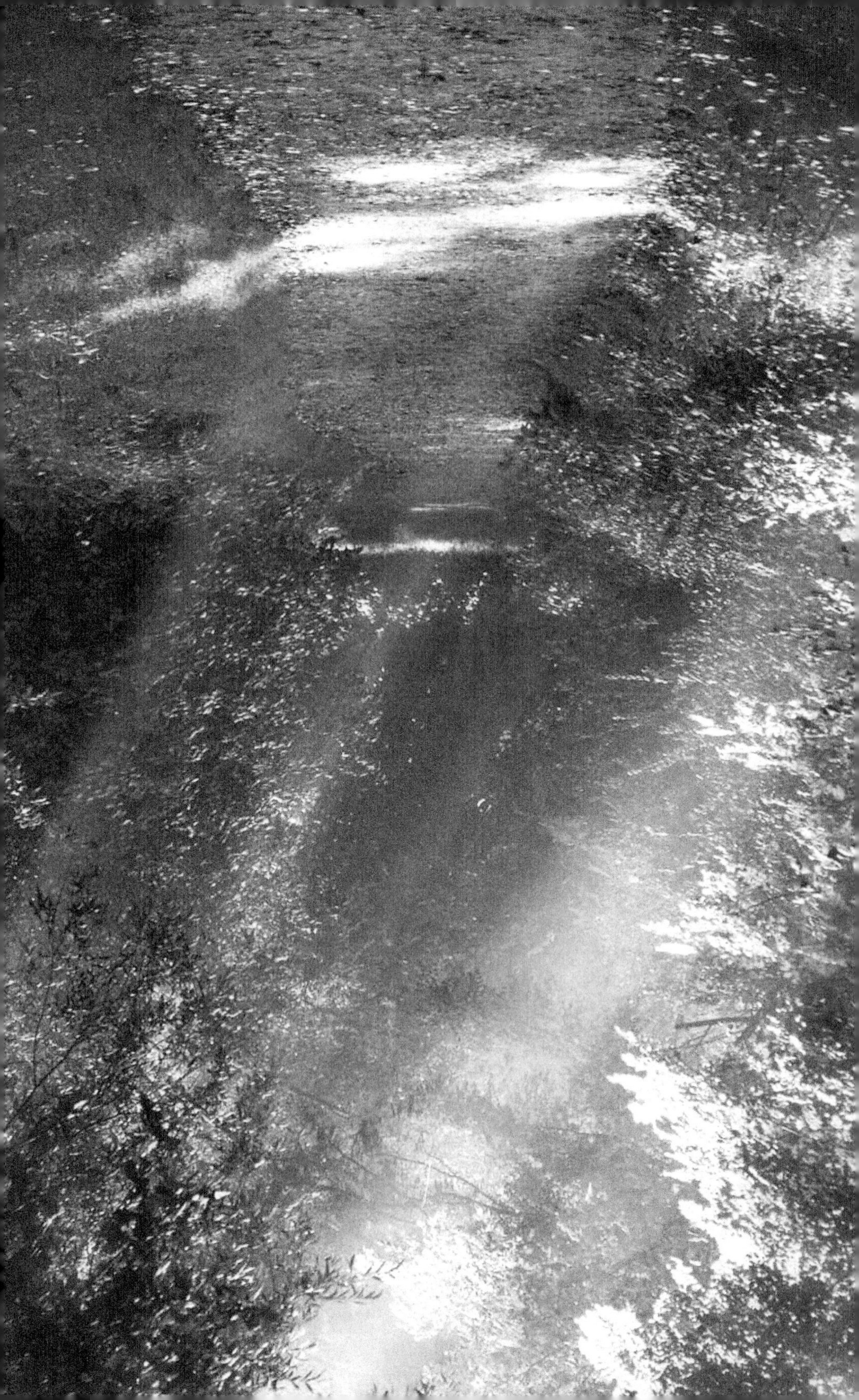

CHAPTER 1
Road to Discovery

This way of living in my business, personal and social life has lead to the most stress-free and successful way of surviving, despite the many difficulties that I have had to deal with. In this book I have laid out the philosophy in the most logical way I could, using my personal experiences for context. Digging deep beyond all indoctrination from family, education, peers, media and social circles, it is important to discover who we really are, then why we are alive and what our meaning and purpose is. We then need to work out what we are going to do to fulfil those meanings and purposes, in what environment we wish to live in to do that and how we are going to achieve it.

Our first task is determine who we really are, to be able to get rid of any 'blind assumptions' and develop the skill of watching what we feed our brain with. Then we are able to determine what we really want from life. True happiness doesn't come from most of what we are being fed as ambition, like money or sex, we only have to look around to see that they are only borne out of desire. Any pleasure is fleeting and often comes with the price of making both ourselves and others suffer. Happiness naturally arises from having a deeper meaning and purpose in life. So how do we determine what that is?

Blind Assumptions

Before we can map out what we want from life and our business, we have to make sure that we're looking from the right perspective. The great Greek philosopher Aristotle once said, "Give me a child until he is seven and I will show you the man." We've probably been indoctrinated by our family, education, peers and media whilst we've not been mindful of it, and we are making 'blind assumptions' about life and what we want.

Breaking in the 70's

These are assumptions that have been given to us while we were open to influence and not being mindful to what we were feeding our brain on and they are assumptions that we think are ours and in fact aren't. I was brought up in a racist, misogynistic, bullying environment that I carried into a very macho working environment without realising it. I would have vehemently denied being any of those things, and it was only when I started to work on mindfulness and could view the emotions and thoughts that were arising, that I could fully appreciate what was sitting deep down inside: I was horrified!

I didn't fit in with my family, my father was a signaller commando and war hero from World War 2 and eventually found a home in the

Prison Service. He set boundaries at home that were too regulated for me; the rest of the family made a good unit but I didn't fit in and as a result I was unhappy, rebelled, and we constantly fell out. Nowadays I would probably have been diagnosed with ADHD.

At school I couldn't pay attention, failed all my exams, received terrible reports and would 'bunk off' whenever possible. While I should have been at school, I started a business with a friend buying cheap goods in the East End warehouses and selling them to 'factory agents' (people selling at work), then taking an 'accommodation address' to do mail order and wholesaling out to shops: we sold everything from toys, to woman's clothing, cheap watches, or whatever was in vogue at the time. We even went round South London pubs selling what we claimed were 'smuggled' watches, when the import restrictions had been recently lifted - all while I should have been studying! At the same time, I was doing two paper rounds, selling newspapers from a stand outside West Norwood train station, pulling the blinds down in the early morning for shops in the high street, running jellied eel stalls in and around the Old Kent Road on a Friday, Saturday and Sunday evening, and chipping the ice out of the freezers for Marks and Spencer in Oxford Street on a Saturday. Reading that back, I must have had ADHD: and at 15 I was convinced that I was going to be a millionaire by the time I was 21! I earned more whilst I should have been at school than when I left and got a job.

I was attracted by money, power and all the things I'd never had growing up and blindly assumed that they were what everyone wanted. I did not for a second realise the power of advertising, TV programming and the reverence that society gives to people that horde wealth whilst others starve and constantly demean those that don't have these things. I hadn't realised that society had been feeding my unguarded mind all this time!

Before planning our life and business structure we have to ensure that our mind is in the right condition to accurately determine what we want. How did I get from a South London 'Del Boy' to effect control over my life?

David Carradine - Kung Fu (1972)

CHAPTER 2
The Shaolin Temple

In 1973 I was training in a hard Karate club and working in the security world. I was young, fit, strong and unbeknown to me, a bully. I had been brought up to deal with everything with violence, the club I trained in was violent and very 'street' self defence oriented and in the security world your reputation hinged on your capacity for violence. Deep down I knew my propensity for it was going to get me into trouble and there was likely a prison sentence waiting.

Bruce Lee was my hero: fuelled by hate, rage, racism and violence he would kill and maim a huge body count (usually consisting of Japanese victims) with an amazing array of Kung Fu skills. Then one Sunday at 3pm the TV programme *Kung Fu* came on and there was this Shaolin priest played by David Carradine, a quiet, humble, spiritual, patient and kind man making his way across America's cowboy west, with an amazing set of Kung Fu skills, only employing them to keep the peace.

There were scenes in between where the screen would go fuzzy and the programme would go back to the past, where he was in the Shaolin Temple as a trainee priest learning Buddhist insight and wisdom from his Masters. I immediately knew this was the path I was destined to follow. I found a Tai Chi teacher who luckily took to an uncouth karateka and would come in early to 'push hands' with me and discuss martial arts. My undisciplined mind was always looking for the distraction and excitement that I found with sparring and fast movement, so I found the slow movements incredibly difficult and frustrating but knew the mental discipline was good for me.

My teacher also gave me a copy of the *Tao Te Ching* by Lao Tsu translated by Jane English and Gia-Fu Feng. I'd never read a book up to this point but the moment I started reading I was spellbound.

"The Tao that can be told is not the eternal Tao.
The name that can be named is not the eternal name.
The nameless is the beginning of heaven and Earth.
The named is the mother of the ten thousand things.
Ever desireless, one can see the mystery.
Ever desiring, one sees the manifestations.
These two spring from the same source but differ in name;
this appears as darkness.
Darkness within darkness.
The gate to all mystery."

It was written in this lovely poetic fashion to give insight to the reader and I immediately understood the philosophy behind it. That brain that western education had failed miserably to educate could take easily to this Eastern, more artistic approach. This led me to a lifetime of studying Taoism, Buddhism and Asian philosophy.

The World of Opposites

What we call the 'yin/yang' symbol is actually the Tai Chi symbol. Not named after the art of Tai Chi (because that is named after the philosophy behind the symbol), but the philosophy of the 'grand ultimate'. Let me explain. The circle around the image has no ends so represents the infinite: this is stillness, silence and everything and nothing at the same time, and therefore represents infinity which by it's very nature cannot be defined - thus 'the way that can be spoken of is not the eternal way'. Because it cannot be explained doesn't mean it can't be experienced.

Inside the circle are the black and white 'fish' shapes, forming a curved line down the middle with a small circle of the other colour in their largest mass. The curved line means that the logo is spinning; it would be straight if there was no motion. When infinity is stirred, motion is created, as is time and every creation inside that has to have an opposite. Thus our defining mind can only recognise something by that opposite. We only know light because it gets dark, hot because of cold, male because of female and so on. Infinity is consciousness, our mind is definitive, like the software on a computer, designed to help us survive day to day, moving around in the world of opposites. Nothing can be completely yin or yang, thus the small circle of the opposite within each mass. Inside every male there is the *animus* of a female, and in every female is the *animus* of a male, a sunny day casts shadows and so on.

Our defined universe has to exist inside infinity and the circle of infinity is joined from top to bottom by the curved line balancing the two opposites. This demonstrates that if we balance the two opposites we open a portal to the infinite, or 'grand ultimate'. This ancient philosophy seems to be validated by quantum physics, which shows that from an apparent vacuum matter and antimatter are created simultaneously from nothingness and then come together to cancel each other out. An ancient philosophy explaining quantum physics and the creation of the universe!

With my wife in the 80's

This is the portal of mindfulness. The art of Tai Chi is named after this philosophy that existed long before the art and this is why we need a soft front supported by a strong back: our front is yin and our back is yang.

Our key to survival is to live inside that portal. To balance life and death. We can only engage fully in life by fully understanding our mortality. To present ourselves to life and others with the yin qualities of good manners, mindfulness, patience, tolerance, empathy and compassion and to support those attributes with the yang qualities of resolve, determination, power and strength. This means that we train the good qualities of both aspects.

Two Become Four

Yin is feminine and yang is masculine, yin is winter and yang is summer, we can easily split that two into four, earth, water, air and fire. Earth is winter, air is spring, fire is summer, and water is autumn. Our personalities are also made up of a mixture of them. Earth people are very practical, but can also be locked into that practicality and not be able to look up and see art and imagination; in the martial arts they can be obsessed with the application of technique and not see the broader benefits of training. They also tend to be the last people at the bar to buy a round of drinks! Air is communication, and air people have lots of ideas and love to talk; in the martial arts they tend to talk about training instead of getting on with it. Fire people burn quickly in temper and emotion, but burn out too easily; in the martial arts they have too much enthusiasm and have to be calmed down to study properly. They are children that never seem to grow up. Water are emotional people, stubborn enough to wear everyone and everything down (remember water can wear away a stone) but they can also be very negative in their approach.

Earth people will say "I do", air people will say "I think", fire people will say "I am" and water people will say "I feel". We are all a mixture of these but as a teacher you can see what is dominant in a student and therefore give them what they need for balance. These four then become eight as we have the 'equinoxes' over the course of the year, marking the halfway point between each other, given that the changes are not sudden but rather subtle. In Chinese culture there is the *I Ching*, which marks 64 changes from yin to yang.

When I was studying Wicca, we learned about the wheel of the year, that marks those eight points of the year and their festivals: the 20th to the 23rd December is Yule, Imbolc is the 1st February, Ostrava is the the 19th to the 22nd March, Beltane is the 1st May, Litha the 19 to the 22nd of June, Lughnasadh the 1st August, Mabon the 21st to the 24th September and Samhain the 1st November. Our meditations would reflect these points and their elements. Each element had it's 'elemental' spirit so that we would absorb ourselves in the element of the season and be around earth (gnome) in winter, air (sylph) in the spring, fire (salamander) in the summer and water (udine) in the autumn. We did that until we could internalise the 'feel' of each one and recognise them intuitively rather than just academically. I found this really helpful to be able to 'intuit' the elemental make up of both people and situations.

The number eight in Chinese culture is considered lucky and the bringer of health, wealth and prosperity. In Buddhism there are eight points on a dharma wheel to reflect the 'Eightfold Path' (more on this later), one of the 'Four Noble Truths'. Also, there are eight directions on a compass.

The Buddhist Ajahn

In the 80's I invited Ajahn Anando from Chithurst Buddhist Monastery to give a lecture to my black belt students at a summer course I was hosting in Brighton - considering his audience, it was probably a brave thing for him to do. He started the lecture asking the students to ask themselves: "Who am I?". The conversation went in this fashion:

Are you your name?
No.
Are your thoughts?
No.
Are you your emotions?
No.
Are you your body?
No.
Then who are you?

Very profound.

I remember that the philosopher Alan Watts said that we were "an aperture through which the universe experiences itself".

We can't look back down our own eyes to see who's looking out, or listen down our ears, to find who's listening. We can't smell who's smelling, or taste who's tasting. We can't bite our own teeth, or even beat our own heart. We can't hold our breath until we die, or stop our heart from beating. Our internal organs work by themselves, until it's time to die. We think we have control, and we may have a little, just not as much as we'd like.

Or do we have any? Who or what is our 'puppeteer'? What is looking out of our eyes? Beating our heart, choosing when we die? When it speaks, can we hear? What language does it use? Can we understand? Can it be named? So many questions.

When we sit still, and our mind is aware and focused, when it is sensitive and intense, then we can understand. Behind the fabric of life, underneath this 'theatre', there is a conversation that doesn't use words. If you're still you can hear it. Your body talks to you, so does much of the rest of the world, in a silent language, that is spoken by the universe and unifies everything.

We can trace our DNA back to the beginning of time. It shows that we've always been here in one form or another; there is a far deeper part of ourselves that we can penetrate if we follow the right lifestyle.

Can you see where I'm going with this? Before we can seek the meaning and purpose of our life and business in it, we need first to determine who and what we are to be able to define it. The best route I found for that, and the one that improved my martial arts most, was mindfulness.

Our dojo Quanyin, the goddess of mercy, healing and compassion

CHAPTER 3
Mindfulness

This determination of meaning and purpose and who we really are can be achieved through the practice of mindfulness. The process is simple - but simple is not always easy. The exercise of mindfulness starts with meditation, sitting, standing, laying or walking so that with persistent practice it can be internalised until it's your natural way of being. Too many people practice it for 30 minutes a day and then for the following 23 and a half hours are mindless: in balance, that just can't work.

Dhammapada verse 21 says:

> Mindfulness is the way to the Deathless (Nibbana); unmindfulness is the way to Death. Those who are mindful do not die; those who are not mindful are as if already dead.

To 'mind' something is to take care of it, so to mind our thoughts emotions and behaviour means that we observe and take care of them applying critical thought. This means that we are able to start sifting what we really think and start acting accordingly: this will have a positive effect not only on us but also on those around us and our environment. The more we do this, the more we can internalise it as a process.

The process we use in the exercise is that deep breathing calms the body, then the emotions, then the mind. Deep breathing requires good posture in order to use the lower abdomen and back to bring the diaphragm down and fully expand the lungs. I will give you the process standing, seated, laying and walking, as this covers all daily activities.

Standing

We use five standing postures: neutral, upper and lower yin, and upper and lower yang. With feet a hip width apart, draw the body to it's full height by raising the crown of the head and then loosen the joints from the ankles upwards, to let the body weight drop into the soft tissue. Position the head on top of the spine by not only pulling up but also by lightly pressing it back, 'as if pressing the neck back against the shirt collar', and place the tongue to the top palate just behind the front teeth. Lightly spiral the feet outward without locking the ankles and knees, to rotate the femur in the hip socket and open the hips. Raise the pelvic floor and tighten the PC (pubococcygeus) muscle to pull the coccyx forward. This forms the bow of the legs and forms the bow at the bottom of the spine, it is bowed at the top by raising the crown of the head and opening the occipital region. Putting arms into the 'gunslinger' pose forms the bow for the arms.

These three bows are then connected and take the weight of body. In yin postures the weight rests in the bows, while in yang postures the bows are bowed to load power into them and raise yang energy up the back. This energy is then drained down the front by softening. Thus the front of the body is soft (yin) and the back strong (yang): this is the physical and energetic manifestation of the soft front and strong back. The body weight rests on the top of the arches of the feet. Left and right and upper and lower regions of the body should be harmonised until they feel the same.

Breathing

Use the lower abdomen and back to breathe, drawing the diaphragm down to make deeper, slower breaths. Breathe out and wait for the body to breathe in of itself. When the body has breathed you in, wait for it to breathe itself out. Repeat the process.

This is teaching you to 'let go' and let the body breathe naturally, without any excess tension or anxiety and without any interference from the mind. It's finding it's own natural healing rhythm. Breathing is the one function that we can control and it is also connected to the parasympathetic nervous system, as we can breathe with or without thinking, and it regulates the internal organs and 'inner health'. We can improve posture, breathing, calm the body, emotions and mind and heal our 'inner self' with this one simple practice.

As the body, emotions and mind calm down, it is a bit like closing the active windows on a computer and you think that nothing will exist, but the background is still there. I often have students that get scared at this stage and think they're going to die, but in fact when all is calm in the stillness and silence, you discover who and what you really are. This is where a hippy might say: "I'm at one with the universe", and that's actually quite accurate. The Buddhists call this 'absorption' and it's in this state that natural insight and wisdom can arise.

When thought kicks back in you lose it, then the harder you try to get it back the further way it goes. To get it back, you simply have to repeat the process and be patient until it is internalised, then you know who you are and are at the right starting point.

Yin and Yang

The 'gunslingers' arms are placed in front of the lower abdomen for lower yin, and in front of the upper body for upper yin, with their weight also resting in the bows. From upper yin, turn the palms outward to the front to make the 'yang' posture and 'sit' the hands backward until in turn it 'sits' the wrists, elbows and shoulders. As you make this action, actively bow the connected three bows I talked about earlier, by pressing backwards through the arches of the feet to match the pressure out of the palms of the hands. For lower yang, lower the arms maintaining the structure until the thumbs point to the mid thigh. Feel the very distinct 'colouring' of the yin and yang energies.

Seated

For the seated version, use exactly the same as standing and either rest your hands on your thighs or use the upper yin and yang arm positions. Sit straight with the knees level with or lower than the hips (a kitchen chair is fine). If your feet are on the floor, you can still rotate them on the floor to open the hips, without the burden of your body weight in them. If your feet don't touch the floor, you can still do the rotation and pelvic floor lift by manipulating your hips.

Laying

Bend your legs so you can place the soles of your feet and the palms of your hands on the floor, and go through everything I instructed for standing. The advantage of laying is the ability for the body to soften down toward the ground and get an energetic return from the ground over a much larger area.

Walking

Again, apply everything from standing and using the unlocking inwards of the leg joints make the minutest circle of the leg as you step. Allow the arms to swing naturally and walk from the waist. Be mindful of balance and feel every part of the foot connect with the ground, walk at a speed that you can notice everything going on in the body and apply this with every step you can during the day.

As a young, very energetic young man with an easily distracted mind, I found these exercises very difficult to begin with. What I realised was that we are all different and it will take as long as it takes. We just have to keep re-establishing mindfulness when we lose it. The two enemies of the mind are laziness and distraction and we don't notice when we slip into either of these states, so when we realise what's happened, it is important to dispassionately re-establish the mindful state without chiding ourselves. This way we don't struggle as much, and the mindless states will gradually dissipate until we can maintain an unbroken state, getting deeper with each meditation and maintaining it longer afterwards, until our life can be one mindful state.

The Computer and the Brain

The software on a computer will evaluate but not store and the hard disk will store but not evaluate. Our thinking mind will evaluate but not store, and our subconscious will store but not evaluate. This is why we can carry so many 'blind assumptions' and indoctrinations from childhood, that without review we would carry for life. If we are unable to be mindful, we will continue to be indoctrinated and manipulated for the rest of our life.

When we activate mindfulness, we are able to view and review our thoughts, emotions and behaviour in an objective manner and the process of finding out who we really are can begin. When we are in a mindful state, natural insight and wisdom will arise, because insight and wisdom cannot be defined, we can only see and describe the results of their application: they belong to the infinite mind that is blocked when lazy or distracted.

With posture and breathing, the mind becomes aware, and that awareness needs to be brought into focus. The focused mind is able to concentrate on itself and scan the body with sensitivity, then that of others and the environment. These qualities need to be guarded by the right kind of intensity, otherwise the mind can easily slip into laziness and distraction and mindless negativity. I constantly remind myself and my students that the qualities of the mind are:

- Aware
- Focused
- Sensitive
- Intense

Using this process, I gradually went from an easily manipulated, over active, distracted, quite violent, troubled youth to a more relaxed, thoughtful, philosophic, compassionate, empathic, vegetarian adult, with a more focused, powerful, resolved and determined mind.

My Karate club became busier with a more diverse student base - from a handful of people to around 4,000 students in various locations run by myself, my wife and other instructors. My association grew to 15,000 members, I became Chairman of the Governing Body of Karate and Operations Manager of a security company with around 500 staff.

This ongoing mindful process helps us to determine who we really are and in turn means that we have the right outlook for what the meaning and purpose our life should be.

The Present is Called the Present Because it's a Gift

When we are in a mindful state, we are fully engaged in the present moment. This truly is a gift. It means that this aware, focused, sensitive and intense mind is able to read ourselves, our environment, others, and what their intentions and strategies are. Most people walk through life blinded by their own thoughts and ambitions, walking past the doors of opportunity and not being able to see how others are perceiving them.

Being able to recognise where we have been causing harm to ourselves, our family, friends, environment and community means that we are able to change those habits and outlooks, and take a path that supports them. This is infinitely rewarding and can not only give a deep meaning and purpose to our lives making us happier, but will also make our success have deep roots building the community and environment around us on a far more permanent basis.

Working in the security company, I was able to grow it having a good relationship with the employees as I could support them and create a happier and more supportive environment for them to work in. A part of my job, however, was also having to entertain clients and that involved large lunches, brandy and cigars, and as a vegetarian, non smoking, hard training martial artist, the lifestyle just didn't suit me. I was finally forging my own path and decided to give up the salary, company car and benefits to be one of the first professional martial arts teachers.

Order and Chaos

For many people it's hard to come to terms with order and chaos. To a human the universe is chaos, and many of us spend our lives battling to conquer this chaos. Every time we manage to exert order over it and feel safe and happy, it throws us a curve ball to disrupt it: unexpected sickness, death, disloyalty from those around us, natural disasters… There are so many unexpected things, because this is the nature of the universe. Those that can only work within structure go to pieces when chaos reigns, and suffer anxiety even from when their structures are working, because deep inside they know that the unexpected can happen at any time.

We need order to structure our normal life, to work, pay bills and do all the everyday 'human' things that we have to do, but this is only half of our life. We have to learn to be as equally at home in chaos, otherwise everything crumbles. Mindfulness helps here, because we are always mindful to the fragility of everyday life and our structures, and we maintain the spontaneity to be able to work within chaos. Martial arts, the Fire Brigade and security work helped me in this, because in combat and in emergencies you have to deal with all problems as they arise.

In everyday life, I maintain a mental image of one foot in life and one in death (the finite and infinite). This way I can work with an awareness of both structure and chaos all of the time. In meditation, I have both feet in death (infinite), with just the little toe of one foot in life (finite). This is my place of refuge and healing.

The Death Meditation

The Buddhists have a death (maranasati) meditation that seems dark to many but in fact is very healthy. By visualising ourselves dying, our body rotting away, how our friends and family are likely to feel and how life will carry on without us enables us to accept death more readily and appreciate and fully engage with every moment we're alive. I do this meditation most days.

Toru Takamizawa and Steve Rowe

CHAPTER 4
The Martial Arts

Going from the security world to full time martial arts, I had also undergone a relationship break up, due mainly to how I'd changed. I actually found myself going from a 3-bedroom house to a 2-roomed flat with a shared bathroom, from a brand new company car to an old banger and from a good salary with expenses to a martial arts club. I was teaching private lessons in student's homes, self defence classes for doctors, nurses, midwives, milkmen, insurance agents, rape crisis groups, WI and adult education groups, and arrest, search and questioning for security personnel. Shortly afterwards, I met my present wife, who eventually trained to 6th Dan Karate black belt standard and has been my partner in crime ever since, helping me to grow our club and association.

At this point I was studying Karate under Toru Takamizawa and Iaido under Okimitsu Fuji. Takamizawa was from a samurai family and had trained in Judo at school and Karate at university. He had studied languages and travelled to the UK with Tatsuo Suzuki, breaking away from him to form the 'Tera Karate Kai' association. Eventually we formed the Takamizawa Institute of Karate, with me being Chairman and representing the group politically. This was how I eventually became Chairman of the Governing Body. I was instrumental in moving him down to Chatham with his family and starting clubs for him. He also taught all my black belt classes. I took private lessons with him for many years. We had to split eventually due to politics from other members but remained good friends until his death. Takamizawa studied science and gave me a very structured approach to studying Karate, physiology and the human brain. He didn't like me studying Buddhism and philosophy but we were great friends and he was a big influence in those areas of my life.

Okimitsu Fuji was the opposite, he was like a 13th century samurai born out of his time. He studied Kendo and Iaido from a very early age after the WW2, and studied with the best instructors from the Miyamoto Shrine Dojo in Japan. His knowledge of Japanese culture and the Budo concepts was very deep and profound. Every Tuesday morning, I would go to his house and wake him up and we would train across the road in the Irish Working Man's Club. I learned so much from him and we became good friends. He named my association Shi Kon (warrior spirit) and drew the calligraphy that hangs on my dojo wall. He knew so much that never occurred to him to teach, but my questioning mind gained a lot of information that helped me to structure my Japanese Zen from a Budo perspective. When he returned to Japan, I started training with Vic Cook in Brighton and took many private lessons with him, also adding Jodo to the system. Vic was an artist and added a lot of missing artistry to my training.

In hindsight, between these two Japanese sensei I had the perfect balance of structure and Zen. Whilst under their instruction, I was also studying Taoism, Zen and Buddhism really intensely which along with my first Tai Chi Sifu helped to form the base of who I am today.

With Okimitsu Fuji, my Iaido instructor

I began teaching self defence to the Czech Police Force, which started a relationship that has spanned over 30 years so far. I also taught in Norway for 16 years, and in Sweden, Denmark, Ireland and Portugal. Whilst in Norway, people recommended that I meet with Jim Uglow, a Hung Gar and Yang Family Tai Chi Sifu. He had a club in East London, so I went to see him and started taking 10 years of private lessons. We became good friends and he took me to Hong Kong to train with Ma Lee Yang, the Yang Family Tai Chi lineage holder, and we made several visits to receive her instruction. I learned a great deal from both teachers, and much about Kung Fu in general and Chinese culture from Jim.

With my Iaido instructor Vic Cook (left) and Aikido's Brian Stockwell (Centre)

The Left Hand Path

By this time I had expanded my philosophical studies to anything that intrigued me. My wife was also an astrology teacher and we studied Wicca, Paganism, became Reiki Masters and would look at anything to do with the mind, energy, meditation and healing.

I was walking the 'left hand path', literally forging a different path to most other martial artists. I was teaching traditional Karate, Tai Chi, Iaido and Jodo, but also realised that what was missing from what I had been taught in the martial arts, and indeed everybody else, was the balancing emotional intelligence and philosophy. Everyone paid lip service to it, advertising the character development of the Arts, but other than overt discipline, had no structure to intelligently incorporate it into their training programme. Japanese Karate was either the post WW2 university sport Karate or 'street self defence' with a lot of negative aggression. Tai Chi was either the hippy health version or instructors were trying to find application that brought it parallel with the Karate street self defence style.

To be effective, I realised that the mind, emotions and body all had to be trained equally and that was what all the original martial arts classics and terminology were implying. Finally my kind of intelligence could be used to structure the training systems. Luckily, many long term practitioners that felt that something was missing in their studies were attracted to my methods, and we've been able to change the face of the martial arts. I had been writing in the martial arts magazines for over 30 years and with the advent of the internet I could spread the word by blogging and social media.

I found myself isolated, however, in the political arena, because there was no one with the same traditional view as me and it was riddled with corruption and self interest. I realised that the interests of martial development couldn't be served inside the Governing Body of Karate, so I resigned my position. It wasn't long before it collapsed into a mire of corruption and we've never really had one since. By this time, I had moved entirely into Tai Chi and Kung Fu and joined the more honourable British Council for Chinese Martial Arts.

I realised that I was trying to keep up the training of too many martial arts. That meant that I would only ever be the 'Jack of all trades and master of none' and that as I was getting older, it was important to structure my valuable training time to gain as much depth as possible. There's a saying in Zen, 'to enter a small door and penetrate deeply', and this has paid off in spades, as the 'bottom line' of all martial arts is the same if you look deeply enough. Another saying is: 'there are many roads up the mountain, but when you reach the top, the view is the same'. This is true of religion and philosophy, and can be applied to many areas of life.

This process formed my base. I'd moved from the perception formed by others as a violent yob and a stupid that would never amount to anything, to finding out that I was nothing like my family, educators and friends, but was in fact highly intelligent, neurologically divergent, with my own very special skill set.

Importantly, looking back, I realise that by starting with mindfulness, losing the opinions and ambitions thrust upon me by others and following a totally individual path of self discovery, all the right doors had opened for me. All the right teachers had appeared at the right time. Although there was no internet in those days, all the right information had come to me from many varied sources and with my divergent brain I had the capacity to put it all together in a way that was unique in my areas of life.

I met a lot of opposition, particularly from those in the martial arts that felt threatened by my presence. As my club, association and reputation grew, there were many attempts to discredit and bully me. A relationship had collapsed with animosity and I had to fight against all odds to get custody of my daughter. I succeeded in all areas because the truth always finally comes out and others dishonesty is eventually shown up.

This put me on to a good road to meet the many challenges ahead.

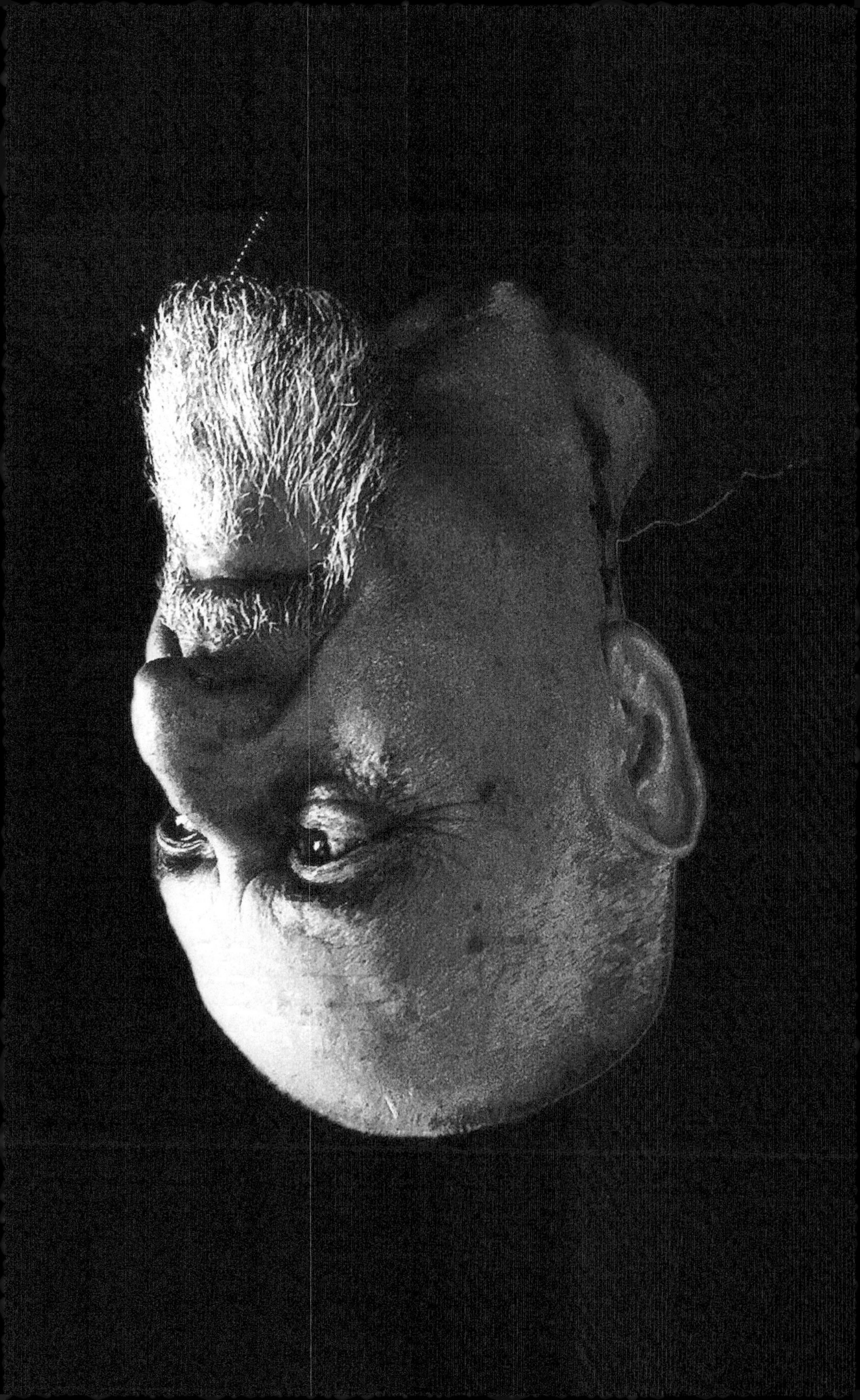

CHAPTER 5

What the Prophets Knew

When we manage to calm the body, emotions and mind, when we find that portal to the infinite containing insight and wisdom, we realise that because infinity cannot be defined, we can't explain exactly what it is to others.

Imagine that someone had never eaten a banana. How do you explain its taste? If they'd never seen one, how can they know for sure whether they exist? When the Buddha became fully enlightened and was on the road, he met some friends that had been spiritual seekers alongside him and when they asked him why he looked so radiant, he told them he was fully enlightened. The reaction was the same as he might get anywhere today: they didn't believe him. This disturbed him and a good friend advised him not to worry because 'some people only have a little dust in their eyes'.

The Buddha, along with Jesus and many of the prophets of the past, couldn't show or explain the infinite that had been revealed to them. They had to rely on stories and allegories to hopefully reveal examples of what insight and wisdom can do, giving the listener a 'glimpse' of the infinite. This has been done down through the ages with sutras, parables, koans and so on, like showing one facet of a many faceted jewel. The prophets could only guide students and followers to discover the infinite for themselves, thus Buddha means 'one who is awake', Guru 'leads a student from darkness into the light', Sensei is 'one that has already made the journey': they can lead by example and teach by 'direct transmission' a teaching that reaches beyond the conscious mind.

Engaging In Life

To fully engage in life, to find that deeper form of happiness, to have a perspective that knows what and who we are, we have to have found the infinite within ourselves. We have to understand our relationship with the present moment, life, death and the universe. We have to understand what our body, emotions and thoughts are, to be able to discipline them for a successful life, and we also have to know what success for us is.

The Triple Jewel

Another excellent 'Triple Jewel' of advice comes from Buddhism, and it is Buddha, Dharma and Sangha. This is my interpretation of them that I think is worth sharing.

Buddha means 'the one who knows' how to penetrate that veil to the infinite, take refuge there and seek insight and wisdom.

Dharma means to search for the truth in all things, including yourself, and your meaning and purpose that is found in that insight and wisdom that resides in pure consciousness.

Sangha means to be around and find support in like-minded people on the same journey.

I found these simple, clear reminders of what my journey is and that a support group, like that which I've developed in my dojo is important because it continually brings me back when I get distracted or lazy.

I can't stress how important keywords have been in my life (I will explain more on this later) and training to keep it simple and to keep me on course.

Relationship

The primary relationship is with ourselves, we use the exercises I've outlined to to build the aware, focused, sensitive and intense qualities of our mind. We build the yin qualities of the soft front with patience, kindness, tolerance and compassion, and we support them with the strong back thanks to resolve, determination, strength and power.

We then need to extend that soft front out to others and our environment. Many people talk about 'love' but I found this a difficult term because I definitely couldn't love everybody and we can 'love' our wife, children, pets, chocolate, car, favourite outfit, perfume and many other diverse things. The use of the word is way too far reaching. But we can have patience and kindness toward everyone, we don't even have to like them! So the Buddhist 'metta' meditation worked for me because once you find patience and kindness toward yourself, you can than extend it out to family, then friends, then acquaintances, then those you feel ambivalent towards, then to those you dislike – and finally toward those you hate! This is quite a long process to extend genuine feelings but it transforms your character and how the others perceive you.

The word *persona* comes from 'person' and 'sonar' and was the masks worn by actors, before microphones were invented, to project their voice and character to an audience. When we wear our persona as a mask, we often think we are hiding what we really feel about people, when in fact they can often see through this mask and know how we really feel. Many of us then go through life wondering why we are unsuccessful and why we have no real friends, not realising that everyone we meet can see through our phoney persona. The metta meditation means that we can resolve this and truly become that better person. People will then take to your genuine personality and want to be friends, supporters and be involved in business you do.

Animation

As I explained earlier, our energy can be made brighter, can be coloured and moved round our body by our mind and intention. As energy rises through areas of the body that are sensitive to areas in our life, this is also representative of how we progress as a human being. These sensitive areas are also known as 'chakras' with the energy changes taking place in an alchemical process. The energy is often referred to as 'chi', 'ki', or 'prana'. The calligraphy for 'chi' represents steam coming off a rice pot: all the components of this energy - food, heat and oxygen - create the energy that animates the body.

The Alchemy

This is my direct experience from my years of martial arts training and healing in a way that I hope you can directly relate to and experience for yourselves. I'll also map out the alchemy and healing of a human being through the practice of the martial arts and how it reflects through the chakras.

I don't 'believe' anything. I either know it because I've experienced it for myself or I don't. This is how I, and in my experience, other people like yourselves, experience energy in your chakras, how you 'read' them in yourself and others and how to effect a level of healing through them.

Chakras are intense energy areas of the body. We experience a lot of our life through them. When we are troubled, they get either more intense or void of energy. Let me explain how.

The Root Chakra is located at the 'root' of the torso, around the genitals and anus. This is the chakra that is tied to the Earth and therefore deals with survival and life and death. We experience the urge for procreation there (sexual feelings), and if we are in mortal fear we definitely feel it there. The energy drive from this area is very powerful and exciting and is known in Kung Fu as 'jing'. Because it's the same exciting energy, sexual urge, surge for domination, survival instincts and death can become confused, and the base instincts can end up controlling our mind and emotions in a deviant fashion. When the energy at the Root Chakra is disciplined and directed by the control of sexual urges (though natural and not necessarily complete abstention, as some would believe) and mortal fear (conquering the fear of death), immense power is realised through the body as it is directed upwards toward the other chakras. This can be seen as 'raising the kundalini' and since it can be a high state of arousal, it is often seen as dangerous. However, as long as the energy is alchemised and once raised up the back (often referred to as the 'governor vessel') and then drained down the front (often referred to as the 'conception vessel'), the bridges between being the tongue to the top palate and the PC muscle in the pelvic floor, it's therapeutic and not dangerous. This is often referred to as the 'microcosmic orbit' or 'heavenly cycle' of energy.

The Sacral Chakra is located in the abdomen, at the centre of the body, in relationship to the gravitational pull of the earth, and it is where we feel our 'gut instincts'. We know the feeling when our mind tells us one thing and our gut instinct tells us another. We might go with our mind, because it's more 'logical', and then regret that we never listened to our instincts. We just 'know' when someone is right or wrong, when a situation is right or wrong and what someone is going to do next. We have to learn to get in touch with our instinctive self to always use it alongside our thinking mind and learn to rely on it. This is not only an essential skill for a martial artist in spontaneous combat but for all of us – as life is spontaneous and our instinctive mind comes from the deepest and most natural part of ourselves. The energy here is known as 'chi'.

Having conquered our fear of death, gained control of our sexual urges and got in touch with our deepest instinctive self, we move on to the Solar Plexus Chakra. This is where we have to deal with anger and fear and the energy is known as 'geng' or 'warrior energy'. It is said that when the energy at this point is well controlled, we become 'warrior and gardener' – able to kill for our country and self-protection, ready then to go home and tend to the roses in the garden. We all feel fear and anger at this point in our body, often called 'worry pains'. This is where we get ulcers and sore spots due to stress and it is where we naturally put our hands when we feel anxious. If treating patients at this point with Reiki, they will often burst into tears or uncontrollable laughter as the energy is released.

This brings us to the Heart Chakra and we all know that we feel love, patience, tolerance and compassion here. These qualities can't really be expressed properly without having gained an element of control over the Root, Sacral and Solar Plexus energies first. This is why, although we are always working on all facets of our life at the same time, there is also an 'alchemical' process taking place.

Developing these qualities means that you are ready to express them to the outside world and this is where the Throat Chakra and communication to others comes in to play. We hear the expression that we 'choke on the words' or experience difficulty in expressing ourselves: this is because of a blockage at the Throat Chakra.

Having now become reasonable human beings that can control our sexual urges, not fearing death, in touch and able to trust our instinctive self, able to control our anger and fear, developing love, patience, tolerance and compassion and being able to express it to the world, the 'spirit world' or the higher aspirations of our mind want to talk to us. This is when the Brow Chakra or 'third eye' becomes more important and the energy turns to 'shen' or 'spiritual energy'.

The 'third eye' gives us inspiration, insight and wisdom from our higher self. As described earlier, this can be through meditation, dreams, visions or instinctive thought and actions. The saying 'when the student is ready, the master appears' is relevant here in that you either find good and inspired people as friends and teachers, or you may just walk into a book shop and just instinctively pick up the right book to read that you need at that moment. If a person opens the third eye too soon (maybe with drugs), they could well be troubled by disturbing dreams, visions and thoughts.

Finally, having understood the energies of life and death, being in touch with our instinctive self, controlling our anger and fear, developing compassion, patience and tolerance, being free enough to let our 'higher self' through to communicate with us, we become a complete human being. This is when the alchemy is complete and it is reflected at the Crown Chakra. All the old sages, from Buddha to Jesus Christ, they are all depicted with a golden light or 'halo' at the Crown Chakra, showing that their alchemy as a human being is complete.

Reiki and Healing Energy

The reason that we have a brain is because we move: we have to be able to anticipate, otherwise we'd be bumping into everything and walking off cliffs! Anything that doesn't move, doesn't have a brain. This 'anticipation', with a developed reflective consciousness, is the gift and curse of humankind. It gives us the ability to think forward and the ability to become unnecessarily anxious and fearful. Clearly, it needs to be treated mindfully.

When we are sensitive to, and can animate, colour and lead this energy in ourselves, we are also able to do it in others. Humans are tribal people and touch, empathy and affection from others is important to us. When we are hurt, the first thing we do is to put our hand to the wounded site and maybe rub or massage it. When a child is hurt, we also do the same and 'rub it better'. Even when emotionally hurt, it is good to receive and give a hug. We are tactile by nature and that is important to us: pain, both physical and emotional, are exacerbated by lack of empathy and touch from others, so we have a natural 'need' for it.

Our personal space is our reach out and touch space, and it is an area that we are highly sensitised to. In this space our brain will work in anticipation of contact, thus, if it is seen as a threat, we will 'flinch' in fear or react with skills that we have learned. This is how I worked out the 'wedge point' in our self defence system that I will talk about later in the book. Similarly, if the contact was from an attractive person from the gender that we like, our brain and body may have different more pleasant reactions, or if both the hand healer and healee have good healing intentions, the brain and body will react 'in healing mode'. The 'energy' that both parties feel is their own anticipation of touch – and although not a 'channelling' of energy as often described, it can be just as powerful.

Some people have a lot of energy and that is not necessarily good, they can be energetic, ADHD, arrogant, nasty, mentally unstable and sick, or they may be calm peaceful, yet powerful people that have worked for emotional intelligence, and learned to control and focus their power with years of hard, correct and powerful training. Look at their character, their lifestyle, their training methods, their students and healing results to judge for yourself.

Some people believe they are 'wounded healers' and 'sacrifice' themselves and their energy to heal others. In my opinion they are just as dangerous, passing on their problems to others. Reiki and the healing arts also has many 'snake oil salesmen', constantly wanting to put themselves on a 'higher spiritual ground' to you and present themselves as 'Channelling Masters' – people that are unable to become anything in the real world, so they live in their own little 'gamers paradise' where they're special and will probably have their hand in your pocket all the way through.

Hand healing is natural. Anyone with good intentions can do it. If one or both people are well trained in mind-body connection and meditation, it can be enhanced. It has a good, sound, scientific base.

The Happy Button

The biggest problem that we still encounter in all of these studies is that due to apathy and distraction, we easily slip into old habits and that often means a miserable mindset, particularly if we are surrounded by unhappy people. I remedied that with the 'happy button', a mythical button in the middle of my chest that I worked on by continually pressing it during the day. We can't hold on to a thought, they come and go; we develop our habits by constantly recreating the same thoughts.

A common Zen saying is that in meditation we should allow thoughts to arise, serve them tea (examine them) and then allow them to leave ('keep both doors open'). By doing this, we can be mindful toward the unhappy ones and the physical action of pressing the happy button reminds us to stay happy. We don't need a reason to be happy as it's a healthy state of being, all we need to do is constantly remind ourselves to maintain the state and we can reinforce this by 'pressing the button'.

If we hurt ourselves, we clean the wound, dress it, care for it, rest it and allow it to heal. If we hurt ourselves emotionally, we often end up doing the opposite and keep wounding ourselves.

The Two Arrows

The Buddha likened it to two arrows. He said that the first arrow is the suffering in life we can't avoid. All the time we have a body, emotions and mind there will be suffering. The second arrow, he said, we can avoid: that is the arrow of suffering about our suffering, being angry about our anger, anxious about our anxiety, scared of being scared. There is no point in increasing the negativity. It is amazing how many people actually pick that arrow up and then repeatedly stab themselves with it!

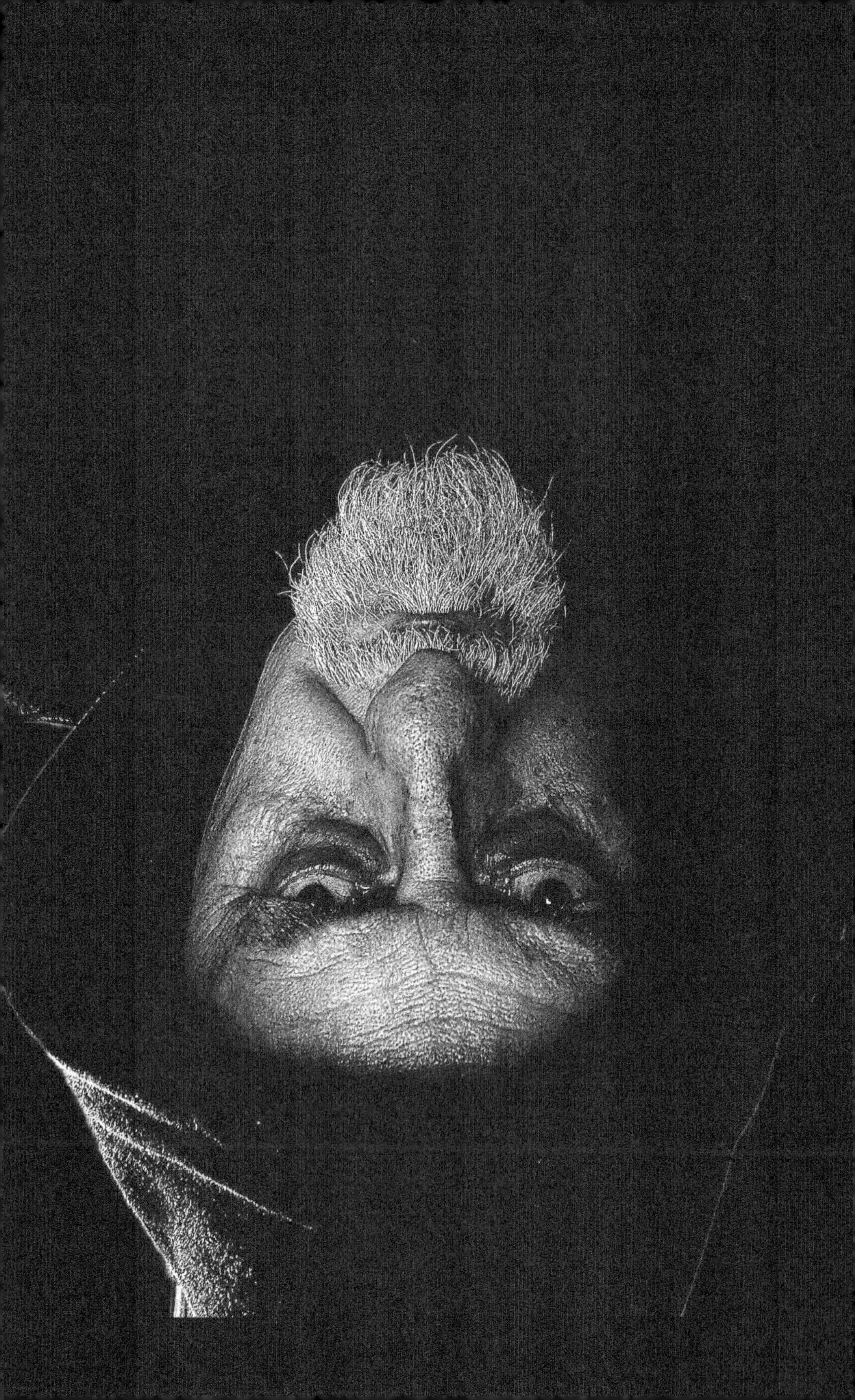

CHAPTER 6
Suffering

Suffering is a fact of life: how can we experience happiness and joy if we don't have anything to compare it with? Dealing with pain and suffering is something that I have a lot of experience with and probably the subject of most advice I have to give. Let me give you some context from my own life.

I injured one knee in the late 70s throwing someone, when their foot got caught in the mats, their knee wrapped around mine as they fell and dislocated it. The meniscus slid out and I had to 'bum walk' to the wall, push it back in and wait for the shock to subside. I went to the GP who made an appointment with a consultant, but it was in a year's time! Of course it had healed by that time but it did get me to take a decision that was to save my life several times in the future, and that was to take out a private medical insurance for myself and my family.

Later the other knee was accidentally stamped on whilst training and these two events were the beginning of many years of pain and suffering. By 2006 I was teaching the Czech police on the 3rd floor of a building with no elevators in Jablonec. I found that due to arthritis in the knees, I had to go up and down the stairs sideways, very slowly, whilst all the students were going past me. That was the point that I knew that I had to do something to remedy it.

I made an appointment to see a consultant and in 2007 he decided that I was strong and fit enough, and with a strong character to endure pain, and was therefore eligible to have both knees replaced at the same time. After the surgery I got home and felt sick: whilst making my way to the toilet, my legs gave way and I fell onto my knees and then backwards (even whilst typing this I still have PTSD from this event). I went into shock with the worst pain I'd ever had in my life. My knees swelled and immediately started bruising, my wife packed them in ice and I stupidly refused to let her call an ambulance. Eventually I could get up and move and since I had a visit to the consultant scheduled, I thought I'd wait for that.

I told the consultant what had happened and that my knees were highly unstable and painful but he arrogantly dismissed me with: "What do you expect, you've had both knees replaced". He then advised me to get more physio. My problem was that I could deal with pain better than most and my sense of balance was very good from my training. Therefore I managed, despite my legs frequently and spontaneously giving way from under me, for another five years before I went to see a different consultant.

He looked at my legs and said: "You don't have any quadriceps on either leg. How an earth can you even stand?". When I had fallen, unbeknown to me, I had torn three of the four quadriceps muscles on both legs and they had disappeared up into my groin. When doing the knee replacements, the surgeon has to cut these muscles and then stitch them back when the knee has been replaced. My previous consultant, despite my constant mentioning, hadn't even bothered to do an ultrasound scan to check whether this had happened. The new consultant referred me to a top orthopaedic surgeon in London to see what could be done about it.

What had happened was apparently unprecedented with knee replacement surgery. This all ended years later with a £1m 6-year court case for negligence against the original surgeon, that I lost because it was found that as there was no previous occurrence of my problem: it was reasonable that the surgeon wouldn't think of doing that ultrasound. The London consultant said that as the muscles had retracted five years earlier, they were probably dead, but if I was up for it he would try to re-attach them. I foolishly agreed and had two long 5-hour surgeries as he tried to re-attach them. Both surgeries failed and in the second one I caught a life-threatening sepsis infection.

That led to months in hospital, the knee being taken out and an antibiotic spacer put in, and a really hard, painful time, but it was nothing compared with what was to come.

In 2015 I was taken ill returning from a summer course in the Czech Republic, collapsing at Gatwick Airport. It took them over an hour to get me into the ambulance as my entire system was crashing and I was in terrible pain, but they finally took me to the NHS hospital in Surrey. The hospital was poorly staffed and I was given a couple of 'wash out' surgeries and then was prepped for a 3rd one that involved some sort of drain being fitted. I knew I wouldn't survive it and had to get out. As luck would have it, my private consultant had just returned from India and was prepared to take me. I couldn't get an ambulance, not even a private one, so in the end I phoned a friend that owned a people carrier, ripped all my tubes out, discharged myself, waited for him outside in a wheelchair and he took me there. Upon arrival, the consultant took my wife and daughter to one side for 'the chat' and said that first, as I was in renal failure, he had to save my life, and then see what he could do about my leg. I was in hospital for 5 months, had several surgeries and ended up having my knee removed and my leg fused straight.

Eventually the bar through my leg started to break through the shin bone and I had my third and probably worst life-threatening sepsis attack. In March 2021, during the covid crisis, I was 'blue-lighted' into Medway A&E for an emergency above-the-knee amputation. I'd now had over twenty-five surgeries, mostly on my legs.

When I came out of hospital, one of the blood tests showed I had prostate cancer. Therefore, in August 2022 I undertook a month of daily radiotherapy and hormone treatment. It was intensive and six months later I am still recovering, probably because of all the problems I had with my legs beforehand.

As I'm sure you can imagine, this is a very shortened account of a long list of incredible pain, suffering, mind and emotion changing medications with twenty-five surgeries, three life threatening sepsis infections, horrific arthritis, an amputation and cancer, with me going from a very fit, strong martial artist to a sick, disabled amputee.

The biggest change in life is when we take responsibility for ourselves. To accept life as it is, to stop blaming other people and events for our unhappiness and misery. It's all down to us, happiness depends on what we are inside; on understanding what we can and can't change, and moving forwards with the right perspective. We have to learn to stop 'blame-throwing' as everyone and everything is as it is. It is no good trying to expect them to change to fit our expectations. It is our expectations that have to become realistic and then we can work with that.

My leg won't grow back, I can't be young again, I have to accept that and not waste time and emotions wanting things to be different. My time and energy need to be spent in something productive. I do my Tai Chi seated twice a day, people come to me rather than me travelling to them. I spend my time doing what I can to fulfil my meaning and purpose for both me and my community. I teach other teachers, helping them with the insight and wisdom that I've gained through my experience. At 73 years old, with one leg, chronic fatigue and arthritis, it would be too easy to turn away from martial arts because I can't do what I used to and not want to be seen as weak and vulnerable. It is a hard pill to swallow, but I teach from a wheelchair using senior students to demonstrate, with all my vulnerabilities on show. People readily accept me for the knowledge I have. My coaching abilities have also improved immeasurably having to explain rather than show.

I recently taught two large seminars for Goju Karate students in Basingstoke, in aid of cancer treatment for two senior Goju teachers. There was 70 mostly senior black belt practitioners and it seemed surreal for me teaching all these, young, strong, fit martial artists from a wheelchair. Because I usually teach Tai Chi in my dojo (I live above it) in small groups, this was a real challenge for me, mainly having to come to terms with my disability and how others see me. I did it, it was highly successful and raised £8,000 for a good cause; it helped me to understand that I can still have value and the way I see myself is not necessarily how others see me. Without testing my view and perspective how am I going to know how accurate it is?

Letting Go

Pick up a stone and hold it in a clenched fist. Now there is two ways you can let it go: the first is with palm downwards you can let it drop to the floor, and the other is with palm upwards you can let it go and keep it suspended in the palm.

Often people think that to 'let go' means to discard and disassociate with everything, but as with the stone, it is not the only way. You can also 'let go' but still fully engage. How can we do that? There is a saying "if you love someone let them go, if they come back it was meant to be, if they don't it was never meant to be". Does that mean that you love them less? No, it means that you love them more because you're allowing them to be what they're meant to be and not trying to indoctrinate them with your wishes. By not imposing ourselves on anyone or anything, we are releasing our hold over them, yet we are still able to fully engage and probably enjoy them even more. It's the palm upward approach.

I sometimes get students that have been hurt by someone say: "That's it, I'm going to become a Buddhist and have no attachment to anyone or anything anymore." The truth is that they are hurt and this is a form of aversion that will only hurt more. Attraction and aversion are just two sides of the same coin of desire - to have and to avoid - both will bring suffering. Non-attachment is to be free from the desire of to have or not have, and to be able to fully engage without suffering those troubles.

If we are going to work on letting go, we have to know exactly what we're letting go of. It makes for a great meditation and act of mindfulness to see what we are attracted and averse to. Every time the desire for either arises, we should 'serve them tea' (examine them) and then let them go. To try and suppress them will only make them worse and give them more energy, whereas to examine them and see what the result will be is to become wise to their influence. Then letting go of them is only natural.

If we'd always wanted a new car, the desire to own when we don't have it is suffering; when we save up and buy it, as soon as we start driving and the mileages starts to clock up, it's no longer new, so that is suffering; it might rain and it starts to get dirty, you might scratch it, that's suffering; every time someone gets in with dirty shoes or with food, you suffer anxiety. If you are beautiful, as you age and your beauty fades, that's suffering, so you see how it's the desire to have, to keep, or not have that causes the suffering.

Impermanence

The only thing that is permanent in this universe is that everything is impermanent. Everything rises from the earth and returns to it. Understanding this is what keeps us sane, you can't hold on to anything. It is like the whole universe is on fire, it is beautiful to watch, to feel the warmth from, but the moment you try to hold on to it, you get burned.

The Tao Te Ching says:

> "The space between Heaven and Earth is like a bellows.
> The shape changes but not the form;
> The more it moves, the more it yields.
> More words count less.
> Hold fast to the centre."

The 'Way' is that wordless, unformed, uncarved block that is the unseen and unrecognised universal consciousness, the infinity that we access through the portal of balancing yin and yang. It pervades everything and it is what is looking out of the eyes of every living being. This is important because it is what sits behind everything we think we are, our body, name, thoughts and emotions. It is a bit like a fish asking what water is. This is the form that keeps changing.

Dealing with Pain and Anxiety

This path through life brought me a lot of physical, emotional and mental pain, depression and anxiety. I was fortunate, however, to have the tools to deal with it. I advise a lot of people, often they will come to me in pain and suffering with depression and anxiety and ask me to teach them to meditate. Meditation and the development of these tools is like any insurance or skill: you can't take out fire insurance when your house is on fire, you can't learn to fight when the fight has started and trying to meditate when in a high state of arousal from anxiety or depression is extremely difficult.

It's better to learn how to meditate when you feel calm, to find a quiet, peaceful place like nature or a temple like environment, to play chants, music or peaceful sounds and maybe burn incense. It is good to find a group of people that are experienced in meditation to help you start. In this kind of environment you have the best chance of finding that 'portal' to the infinite. You can then create your mindful state in different locations and situations, until you can hold the state throughout the day in situations that would otherwise be stressful. This gradual build up is the best approach. I found martial arts a great environment to stress test my mindfulness with someone attacking me, often with a weapon. Responding to those emergency situations in the Fire Brigade and security world were also a great pressure test. But they were all nothing compared to the surgeries, sepsis, amputation and cancer.

Waiting to go down for surgery is one thing, waiting to go down with a raging infection for major surgery, not knowing if you'll come out alive is another. Sitting on the edge of the bed using mindfulness, understanding that this could be the end of your life, means that you have to draw from the full range of deep, slow, breathing, calming body, emotions and mind, acceptance of whatever is going to happen and then yielding your life to the surgeons, nurses and anaesthetist. In pre-op, you know they're trying to distract you while fitting the cannula and preparing everything, finding the vein (always difficult with me), flushing and then the anaesthetist says "goodnight" and you're gone. The next thing you know you're being woken up with blood pressure and oxygen tests and hopefully a cup of tea and a biscuit.

One time I nearly died in recovery because the morphine had compromised my breathing, and that desperate effort of trying to breathe still troubles me now years later whenever I have any breathing difficulties. The PTSD from that first fall, not being able to breathe post-op, the anxiety about how quickly infection can take a hold and become life threatening, and waking up with no leg are still there sitting somewhere in the back of my being. They are 'dealt with' as they arise, but never fully go away. But I'll explain this more later.

Because of my sensitivity to morphine, two of my major surgeries had to be done whilst I was awake with spinal anaesthesia. That was really strange! Sitting bent over in pre-op, whilst they injected into my spine was strange enough, but it acted so quickly I couldn't get my legs back up on the trolley! Being paralysed from the waist down was really weird. In one surgery they had to remove my knee, effectively cutting my leg in half, removing the spike that held the metal knee in and then fit the prosthetic that fused my leg with a bar that went through the bone from mid thigh to mid shin. This was done quite violently, while I watched, with a hammer, chisel and electric drill. I couldn't feel what they were doing other than my entire body shaking as they hammered and drilled, and in my meditative state it was like they weren't doing it to me. They were all wearing hazmat suits and were absolutely covered in gore as was the entire theatre including the lights that I was looking up at.

Fear and anxiety claw at your guts, they hit you when you don't expect it, which is why you need to be prepared and be able to recognise where possible their incipient stages, because the earlier you can deal with it, the easier it is. When you mindlessly become the fear, you're lost to it.

When I had my leg amputated, it was that or die. There were the difficulties of the infection, my weakened immune system, the fact that they had to remove the bar that was inside the bone more than halfway up the middle of my thighbone; also they would normally wrap the quadriceps muscles around the stump and I didn't have any. I was also 'blue-lighted' into the NHS Medway Hospital mid covid. You can imagine how that made me feel.

The surgery team did a brilliant job, the day nurse team on the ward did the best they could under terrible circumstances, while the night team were all 'bank' nurses bought in from agencies and did a terrible job. I couldn't see any visitors, didn't have a great time and certainly saw life, suffering and death at it's worst! This is why I strongly support a properly funded and well run NHS whatever the cost, because it's where we all end up at some time in our life and watching so many people suffer and die unnecessarily because of lack of funding, staffing and administration is horrifying. And don't forget my other stay in 2015 in Surrey hospital that I had to escape from to save my life.

Steve Rowe

Nothing can prepare you psychologically for losing a limb. You come out of the anaesthetic and only remember what's happened when you look down. I have to admit that I would always feel a kind of shock whenever I realised someone had a limb missing, so imagine how I felt when it was me. If you'd asked me previously whether I'd rather die than lose a leg, I would have said die. And now here I am. The sense of loss is traumatic. The problem is that you don't just feel this once, it happens every day. When I dream I have both legs, when I wake up I forget that it's not there and every morning I suffer that loss all over again. During the day I forget and then remember: two years later I'm still doing this. To cope, each time I have to go through the process of acceptance, this is who I am now. I'm not the man I was before, that time has gone and won't be back. People look at you differently, they talk to you differently, they don't even know they're doing it.

You have to kill the previous you off, you can't go back there, that person doesn't exist anymore. Of course it's a bitter pill to swallow but this is learning to live in the present, the past doesn't exist or the future, the more fully you can exist in the present moment, the less you will suffer. The past is something to learn from and the future only has possibilities, but even that will only be partly due to what you do in the present and how you develop the ability to spontaneously respond to it.

For me, anger is the hardest to deal with. The frustration of not being able to do things for myself. To be in an environment where I have to rely on other people for everyday things, to be a burden on others, the guilt and anger can be overwhelming. I can't continually ask for help, I'd rather do without, the pain is less. There are many times I'd rather be dead and it is not the disability, pain or sickness, but the burden of having to ask others for help and not being able to do things for myself, that lack of independence.

To cope with this, I have to take refuge in the infinite to give me balance. At least twice a day I have to meditate and practice Tai Chi. I wouldn't have survived without all that previous training. I have to let go of so much, that if I was only starting to learn now, I probably couldn't do it.

Soft Font Strong Back

For all the trouble that I'd had in my life, it was nothing compared to what's happened since that first fall, post surgery in 2007 until now. My martial art training, the meditation, the study of philosophy in Buddhism, Taoism and Zen is what has kept me sane. All this raises the question would I have rather had an easy life? One part of me says well yes of course, but then I realise how much these challenges have taught me and changed me as a person. Without them I probably would have spent my life as an arrogant idiot thinking I had all the answers, not realising that they weren't even my opinions in the first place! I look around at some of my friends that have had an easy ride and some that are very rich financially, and I certainly wouldn't want to be them! The bigger the challenges, the more you grow. I was not a nice person in my youth, not sure I can say I am now, but I'm certainly a lot more patient, kind, empathic and stronger than I was.

I remember listening to a Buddhist priest on Terry Wogan's *Thought For The Day* on Radio 2 many years ago. He said that his friends would tell him: "All that meditation you do, yet you still can't control your temper!. He would answer: "You should have seen me before I started meditating!". I can relate to that.

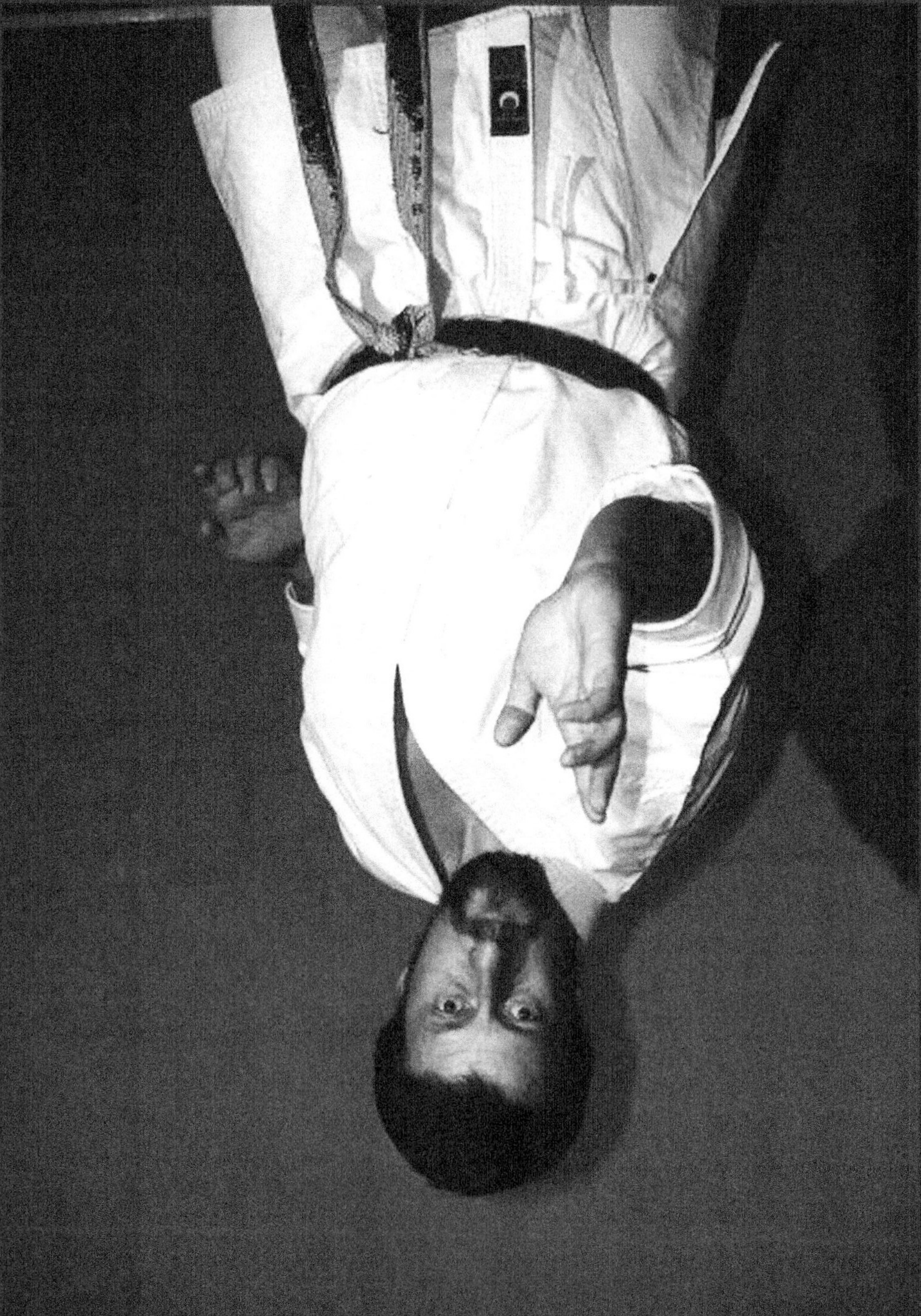

CHAPTER 7
Dealing with Violence

There's always a lot opinions voiced about dealing with violence. Unfortunately a lot of them come from those who have not had enough direct experience and are often frightened and obsessed with it, or have let their testosterone get the better of them.

A famous saying comes from Gichin Funakoshi, the founder of modern Karate, who changed the original kanji that read 'Chinese Hand' to a different one that sounded the same but meant 'Empty Hand'. 'Te' means 'hand' but is used generically to mean 'martial arts', 'kara' means 'empty', as in the 'kara' of 'karaoke' (empty orchestra). The 'empty' is meant in the Zen sense as 'empty of aggression'. Funakoshi also added the ideogram 'do', to make it 'karate-do', meaning 'the Way of the Empty Hand'. 'Do' in Japanese is the same as 'Tao' in Chinese, or 'the Way' as I described in relation to yin yang or Tai Chi symbol. He also wrote *Karate ni sente nashi*, 'there is no first attack in karate', a saying that is constantly being used and abused by many modern day martial artists. When you look at the names and terminology used in traditional Karate, or indeed other traditional arts, you see the same philosophical and cultural references arise again and again. Notice how most of them also attach the suffix of 'do' at the end of their name as well. 'Judo' (the Way of softness), 'Aikido' (the Way of becoming a person of harmony), Iaido (learning the Way through the sword, same as 'Kendo'), 'Wado' (the Way of peace), 'Budo', the generic term for Japanese martial arts that means 'to stop the spear', or to 'prevent violence. The term 'Wushu' for Chinese martial Arts means the same as 'Budo'.

'No first attack' meant to maintain a powerful, balanced, responsive mind with no intention to attack. It is a better strategy to deal with violence with this attitude: the 'soft front', or 'soft skills', as they are known in the security trade, supported by the 'strong back' if needed. To be polite, courteous and sympathetic at first is the better approach, particularly in this day and age where everyone has a phone camera and CCTV is everywhere. The 'pre-emptive strike' constantly advised by others on social media is really not a good idea. The old Kung Fu names for Tai Chi Chuan are 'Soft Cotton Boxing' and 'Deceptive Boxing', meaning that the opponent's attack is met with the soft approach of "stick, blend, follow and disrupt", which, as you can see, follows the names and strategies given to all the other traditional arts. This also means that you can gauge the intensity and skill level of the attacker and negate it with the appropriate response. It would be more accurate to call a traditional martial artist a 'peacemaker' as their function is to negate violence and promote or re-establish peace and harmony.

In Tai Chi there is also the maxim of 'no collapses, extensions or leaning', meaning that any of these will give the attacker the advantage. If you attack first, you will be giving an 'extension' that a skilled opponent will take advantage of. All traditional arts utilise both hands in every technique, it was only when sport was introduced that western-style boxing 'single hand extensions' started to be used. Known as 'husband and wife' hands, the wife/yin hand would meet with softness, to stick, blend and redirect, weakening the opponent's structure, while the husband/yang hand would deliver the necessary punishment.

How This Relates to Life

We have already covered how the idea of the soft front and strong back can be applied to life, but it is worth discussing the idea of 'no first attack' and 'no extensions, collapses and leaning'. It is common sense to not attack people and businesses because you feel threatened by them. How many martial art club owners attack their competition because they feel threatened by them or simply because they're not like them? I have always found it beneficial to work with local martial art clubs, because combined we can increase local exposure to potential students and not look like a bunch of narcissistic and small-minded people. If we are good at what we do, we are bound to be attacked by others on social media and those people only end up looking stupid when we don't respond. Remember the maxim 'don't wrestle with a pig, because you'll get covered in shit and the pig will love it'. However you feel, it's never worth bringing yourself down to their level. Have patience, continue to be the better person and as Winston Churchill famously said:

> You will never reach your destination if you stop and throw stones at every dog that barks.

When I worked in security, in reviewing a business, its property, structure and working practices, however much they boasted about their good points, my job was to think like an enemy and find their weaknesses. The first training session I went on was with the Swedish company Group 4, that at the time had only just moved their business into the UK. The trainer said that 10% of people were completely honest and could never be tempted to steal, however much was offered, 10% were totally criminal and would try to steal whatever you did, while for 80% it would depend on the security measures in place. I have found this to be true and have been able to take those percentages into a lot of other areas in life; they can for instance be applied to violent people, friendship or fidelity in a relationship.

In life and in business you are only ever as strong as your weakest point; it is important to maintain your personal and business structural integrity. You can also spot the weakness in others if they overextend, it could be financially or in their attack. The same with collapsing, it might be in their structure, personnel or practices, while leaning has to do with losing your 'root' and stability. This, for instance, could be in your mission statement and *raison de être*: it is important that you constantly review both your personal and business life, that you have no weak points and that you can see or sense them in others. Part of the genius of Tai Chi is that you start by learning what to do until you are able to see what not to do, which is a neat segway into the learning process.

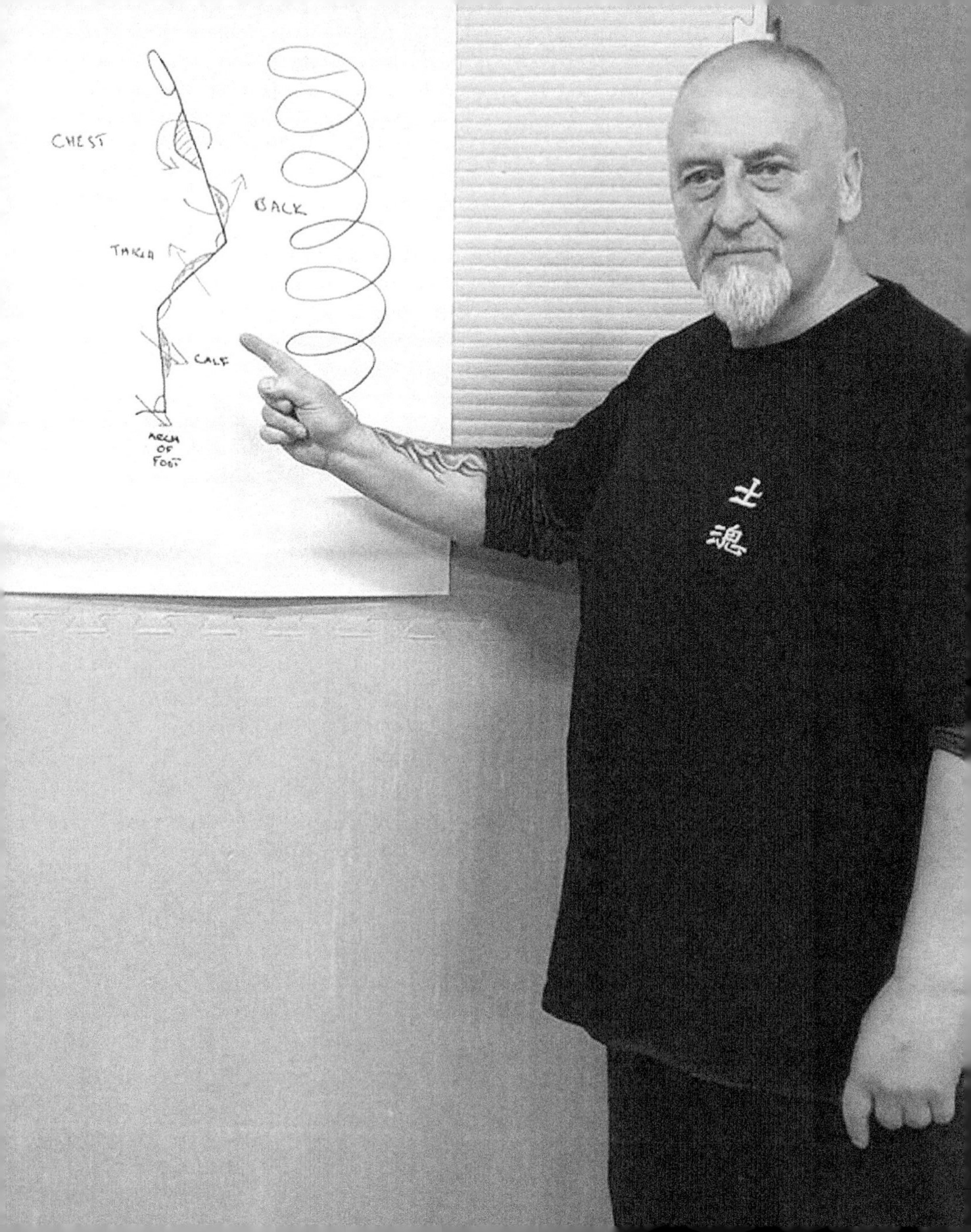
CHEST
BACK
THIGH
CALF
ARCH OF FOOT

CHAPTER 8

The Learning Process

For my trainee coaches, I produced the acronym ATARC: this stands for 'attitude, thought, action, reflection and correction. That is the order, because we first have to teach the student how to learn. The bow at the door of a 'dojo' (do is the way, as explained previously, and jo means place, so 'place of learning the way') is to set the student's attitude and clear the mind ready to learn. If the attitude is not that of a positive, 'willing to learn' one, then nothing will work. Attitude and perspective are aspects of our character that we need to review each day. Thought is planning: if we haven't planned properly what to do, how will it ever work? Action is pure and should be the unencumbered result of attitude and thought. Reflection is the review of what you have just done and whether it matched attitude and thought. Correction is to put right anything that didn't match. It is important to correct in the right manner: if in a movement you place the left foot in the wrong place, you shouldn't assume the correct position by moving the right foot (a common error), because you will have corrected the wrong side of the brain. It is also quite likely that next time you will still put the left foot in the wrong position but will also move the right one, as that is what you will have taught yourself.

ATARC will stand you in good stead for any task in life. The wrong attitude will ruin any task before you start; as per thought, the adages 'proper planning will prevent piss poor performance' (known as the six P's) and 'measure twice, cut once' are good advice. Your plan must come from a good source, the reason why I always found the best coaches, took copious notes, asked many questions and constantly took private lessons, to make sure that I didn't waste any time or be misinformed. If your attitude is good, your action will be pure, unencumbered by fear or anxiety, and you'll be carrying out the task that you had planned. Reflection should not be encumbered by guilt, but with the approach to ensure that you did what you had planned. I can't count the amount of times that a student, when corrected, said things like "I try really hard" or "It's always better at home" or "It's more difficult with you watching", or make countless other excuses. There is no point in excuses or in berating yourself, you are there to learn. This means that you didn't set your attitude right in the first place. Correction is essential for improvement, there is no harm in admitting to yourself and others that you need to correct what you have done, it is also setting a good example for them.

Use of Acronyms and Keywords

Using another brain/computer analogy, I remember Toru Takamizawa saying that the brain is like a computer, in that you can press one key and a screen full of information will come up. This works on a lot of different levels; we use acronyms like ATARC and keywords for this purpose. On the wall in my dojo, we have the eight principles of my Kung Fu expressed as keywords. They are:

- Feet
- Posture
- Mind
- Breath
- Internal
- Power
- Wedge
- Spiral

All eight need to be in place for a technique to work well, and each word is a doorway of exploration for the student when working out what to train on at home, or for a coach wondering what to teach a class: they would only have to pick a word and focus on that area of study.

Feet will correct distance, angle, body alignment, mobility, direction of power and will move the body weight into the technique and are the first 'pumps of chi', as the weight goes in and out of the arches, pumping them.

Posture alignment is essential for balance and structural integrity.

The mind we know has to be aware, focused, sensitive and intense; each one of those qualities is also an entire area of study.

We talked about breathing in the standing postures, and in movement it must be hidden, through the nose, and not betrayed by the chest. A third of the breath needs to be maintained in combat and training at all times. When control is lost the student will lose control of the 'fight or flight mechanism' and will go emotionally from hunter to victim. He will chest-breathe, losing connection of upper and lower body, mouth-breathe, his jaw will drop open, his skin pallor will drain and eyes will lose intent: all signs for the opponent to go in for the kill.

The internal mechanism for spine power is essential, the spine must remain aligned and flexible. It is controlled by the core and the core connects the entire myofascial net. The three bows we discussed in the standing postures work the pumps of the internal system; the pumps are the arches of the feet, the lower back, in between the shoulder blades and the occipital point. When all of this is present along with the mental intention, internal power can be utilised. The spine is like the mast of a ship and the myofascia the rigging, if you plucked the rigging, it wouldn't see much power, but if you bowed the bows and released, or stretched or twisted the spine and released, it would carry far greater power.

Power from the internal system, from use of movement, body weight, structure and intention are primal. In a fight, strategy, venom and power usually overrule all else. Often this gets lost in training.

Wedge is controlling distance, centreline and structure. Personal space plays an important role in that it is important for a student to know when, why and how to react. I teach that we own our body and personal space and it is important to not let anybody into that space or to touch us, unless we want them to. Most people say: "It all happened too fast", because they didn't know when or how to react. Our personal space is our 'reach out and touch' distance. Our senses are heightened when anyone enters that space: if anyone is trying to enter and we are unsure, this is when to act. At this distance our arm has structural integrity and can carry power. Depending on who it is and what is happening, this interception can be just a touch, indexing the person with, "Stop there", "What are you doing?", or "What do you want", to take control of the situation. Or maybe "Stop", "I don't like it", "I feel uncomfortable", together with a touch, and up to a strike, lock, throw, choke or strangle, if required.

In Kung Fu this is known as the 'jeet' (intercepting) point and the angle of the hands as 'child prays to Buddha'. At the shrine, adults will hold incense to their forehead, whereas a child holds their hands together at midway so they can look around and see what's going on. In the praying position, the fingertips are on the centreline. The tips of the fingers form the 'wedge point', where they can intercept the attacking limb of the opponent and wedge in like the prow of a ship cutting through the waves. That wedging hand can slip straight through to a strike, or rotate into a deflection, lock, throw, strangle or choke.

Spiral

A curved, spiralling motion with structural integrity, with no protrusions, collapses or leaning will deflect any incoming attack and power a response. From the Tai Chi symbol we know it is the fundamental power of the universe and has continuous motion and fluidity. Linear movement is empty, weak and only has power at the end, whereas a spiral has no weak points.

It doesn't matter what martial art or style we practice, these eight principles still apply. To defeat an opponent, take one away and it won't work; if all eight are present, it will. Take one away and watch the rest collapse. In any other area of life, particularly business, they still apply: make your root (your mission statement) and ability to move strong (feet); make your structural integrity strong (posture); your ideas need to be positive and innovative with awareness, focus, sensitivity and intensity (mind); life and energy need to have drive and be 'alive' (breath); the whole structure needs to be connected (internal), it needs to be properly funded in all manner of ways and everything needs synergy (power); it needs focus with meaning and purpose (wedge) and it needs a natural propulsion that returns all efforts back to the source (spiral).

The Bodycore Skills

When I am talking about the bodycore, I am referring to the spine and the myofascial line known as the 'Deep Front Line', that connects from the sides of the head down to the arches of the feet. It manipulates the spine and the vagus nerve that controls the parasympathetic nervous system. These three work together and are essential for our health, well being and power. Our 'internal mechanism' is to train them. There are eight skills that we have to recognise and learn to control. They are:

- Soften
- Connect
- Open
- Close
- Stretch
- Compress
- Twist
- Release

Soften is to release all excessive tension, while connect is a function of the mind, which means that you are aware of the connection from the head to the feet, the entire deep front line. Open and close are passive, in that that they are the precursors to power: once softened, the tissue can close toward compress, or open toward stretch. It is important to be able to identify and use these, so that you don't try to compress or stretch too early and create excessive tension. Compress, stretch and twist are methods to build potential energy in the deep front line, as well as manipulating the spine, and release is when you release them to transmit that stored energy.

The above can be applied as a strategy to business and projects. Soften is the courteous communication; connect is everything related to that

Steve Rowe

communicative chain; open and close are the soft preparation for things like funding, getting the ideas out there to prepare the ground; compress is to withdraw to build power; stretch is to open up to build power; twist is to build power through confusion, and release is to then allow it all happen and settle in its new state.

Let's look at some more keywords and their power.

On the whiteboard in my dojo, there are these keywords that we use as a mantra for our Tai Chi.

- Skeleton
- Bodysuit
- Breathing
- Bows
- Yin/Yang
- Sink, Swallow, Float, Spit

Although I have already talked about three of these, I would like to add to the knowledge by looking at them in a slightly different way.

Using the skeleton, we need the bones to balance on each other until good posture makes us feel almost weightless. When you look at the human body, you will notice that we used to be quadrupeds, so our soft and vulnerable underbelly needs to be sunk, 'closed' and protected and our back raised and open, even more so when under threat. If you cut the body down the centre, left and right are identical; if you cut it transversely upper and lower are very much the same. However, for us to move as a quadruped, elbows and knees function in opposite directions to bow and open the spine (see how this fits with the core skills I described); hips and shoulders also work in opposite directions to bow the spine. It is said that many of the vulnerabilities we feel came about when we stood upright to expose our underbelly to our opponents. You only have to look at our protective body language to see this in action.

Then we need to look at the joints. The head (where it sits on the spine), shoulders, elbows, wrists, hips, knees and ankles are known as the 'Seven Stars' of the body, as they give us most kinaesthetic information as to where our body is in space. To make them function well, we need to loosen the body in this order – ankles, knees, hips, back, shoulders, head, elbows and wrists. This enables us to 'sink' our body weight into the soft tissue, to give us a root and mobilise better. We then need to balance or 'harmonise' left and right by making both feet feel the same; the weight should be on the top centre of the arches, then ankles, knees, hips, shoulders, elbows and wrists. After we need to connect or 'harmonise' upper and lower body by mentally connecting feet and hands, ankles and wrists, knees and elbows and hips and shoulders. This is left and right and upper and lower body harmony.

Most physical trainers tend to isolate muscles, whereas we see the body more functionally and consider all the myofascia as one muscle and as a 'bodysuit'. We want the joints to be loose and open, and the bodysuit to have an 'active' stretch: that means lightly, mindfully and actively stretched to open all the tissue and allow the free flow of oxygen, blood, neurology and lymph. That is how we are 'aware' of the entire body, its balance and where it is in space.

We have already covered breathing above, but what I would like to address now is what we call the 'dantian point' ('seika tanden' in Japanese Budo). This is the centre point located in the middle of the body, around three fingers width down from our belly button and it is our relationship with the gravitational pull of the earth. If we move from there, our body moves as a single unit and our weight goes with it. When we breathe from there it pulls the diaphragm down and enables that deeper breathing.

I have already explained the bows quite extensively, but I will make the point here that in the arm-bow the thumbs connect through the chest and the little fingers through the back, the big toes through the inside of the legs and the little toes through the outside. There are actually three small bows in the spine, as some parts are for mobility and some for stability. The three bows are in the lower back, in between the shoulders and at the neck.

With regard to the yin and yang in the body, it is important to understand the concepts, as they can be applied to everything and in a variety of ways: for instance, the front of the body is yin, the back is yang; the lower body is yang (it is where the power comes from) and the upper is yin (power comes from the feet, it is manipulated by the waist and discharged through the hands); the inside of the limbs is yin and the outside is yang.

I added 'sink, swallow, float and spit', a common saying in Karate that I feel it describes the internal mechanism really well and in a way that is relatable. Sink is soften and connect, swallow is compress and release, float is the vacuum it creates for the free passage of energy and spit is the transmission of energy into the opponent.

Memory Palaces

Memory palaces are another commonly used method of remembering. I find them particularly useful for fleshing out keywords and remembering everything to do with each technique in my Tai Chi forms. Every keyword or technique in the form opens a door in the palace. In that room we store all the information we know about that word or technique. It's like pressing the key on the computer I mentioned earlier to bring up the screen of information, but more visual and imaginative. By putting the information in a room, it makes us remember all the facts more easily; we can visualise being in the room and picking up all the facts like ornaments.

I'm often asked how I can do so many seminars or lectures without notes or 'PowerPoint' presentations, and the truth is that I only need to go to a keyword or technique and I'm in that room: I can visually walk around and pick up everything I placed there. My normal memory is awful, I walk into a room at home and forget why I walked in there. I can't remember anything about a movie the moment it finishes… When we used to go to Blockbusters to get movies to rent, I used to come home with the same movies every time! I can't remember people or names; when I am out with the wife and we meet someone and talk for around 30 minutes, as we walk away the wife says: "You haven't a clue who that was, do you" and I answer "Nope…"

I can remember numbers and number plates with stories. 0 is a female, 1 is a male, 2 is a swan, 3 is a bum, 4 is a golf flag, 5 is a cup hook, 6 is a cherry, 7 is a blade, 8 is a pair of glasses, 9 is an upside down cherry, the more ridiculous the story, the easier it is to remember. Letters are the first letters of words. My current number plate is GJ 20 OMR (Go Ju 200 MR).

Keywords, memory palaces and stories work really well when I need to remember. It is like they are all jumbled up in my brain in no particular order, but they always order themselves on the way out. The moment I start teaching or lecturing, as long as I don't try to think, my brain does it all for me.

SHI KON MARTIAL ARTS

We are a class for all

KUNG FU KIDS & ADULTS
PRIVATE TUITION | LADIES KICKBOXING
TAI CHI

www.shikonmartialarts.com 07781 301190

WELCOME TO

KUNG FU KIDS (4-8 & 8+ YEARS)
ADULT MARTIAL ARTS
TAI CHI
LADIES KICKBOXING
24 HOUR DOOR CODE
INSIDE DOJO

HEALTHY LIFESTYLE

FITNESS
SELF DEFENCE
CONFIDENCE
ANTI BULLYING
FOCUS
CONFIDENCE

CHAPTER 9

The Dojo

This brings me to my dojo and training program, both of which are important subjects in my development. As I said earlier, when I formed my own association, my own clubs grew to over 4000 students spread over several locations. I could rely on a group of instructors that over many years I had taught all the way up from beginner level, and an association of around 15,000 students run by instructors that had joined me mainly because of my philosophy and they knew that they weren't going to be bullied or ripped off by me.

This meant that I needed an office and storeroom as a base and for all the equipment. My accountant rented me the offices above his in Luton Rd, Chatham, and that worked until we needed more room, better parking and a shop. We managed to rent a historic part of Aylesford with a shop at the front, offices at the rear and then we also rented a training room for small classes behind that. As we continued to grow, we kept an eye out for a full time dojo, and I found what is now our dojo on Chatham Hill. I love to teach, train and meditate in a place with history: this is a short history of the building that became our dojo. It was written by Brian Joyce and appeared in the Medway Chronicle:

An Uphill Struggle by Brian Joyce

> Readers familiar with Chatham Hill will be aware of the martial arts centre part way up on the southwest side. What they perhaps don't know is that the site was used for religious purposes for about two hundred years.
> In the early nineteenth century, the families living on the Hill had a dubious reputation. Looking back in 1873, the Chatham Observer felt that: "there has always been... a moral element on Chatham Hill very difficult to subjugate; a wild, fitful, bohemian sort of spirit,

often breaking out unexpectedly and requiring a large amount of tact and patience to deal with it.

Some of the more respectable residents of Chatham felt that the people of the Hill were in need of salvation. In 1812, the daughter of the Reverend Slatterie of the Ebenezer Congregational Church, together with like minded friends, rented a room in a cottage on Chatham Hill with the aim of setting up a Sunday School to civilise the area's children. Their efforts prospered, and they were soon in need of more space.

A meeting of prominent Congregationalists in 1813 decided to build a chapel on Chatham Hill. Congregationalist businessmen donated timber and iron for the new building. Others gave money. The new chapel was dedicated in July 1813 on land that some claimed had been used by followers of the prophetess Joanna Southcott some years before.

Forty years later, the Religious Census of 1851 revealed that the Sunday School was also used for adult worship in the evenings. Thirty-two people attended on census day. Earlier that day, sixty scholars attended in the morning, and seventy-three in the afternoon session.

By 1873, this chapel had become dilapidated and uneconomic to repair. A new building was required, and it was the Young family – prominent Congregationalists who lived in a large detached house on Luton Road, that provided the wherewithal.

Joseph Young was a High Street grocer. His younger son had died in 1868, leaving £35 10s to the Chatham Hill Sunday School. Another son was an architect who drew up the plans free. One of the Sunday School teachers was Young's daughter Annie, an important local feminist.

The brick built chapel stood more or less on the site of the previous one. It cost nearly £500 to build and furnish, nearly half of which was still outstanding when the building opened in 1873. It was constructed by the builder William Ruby of Chatham. A large ground floor room that could seat 200 people was used for the Sunday School and adult worship. Underneath was a classroom for infants. The building contained an additional two classrooms.

The chapel of 1873 proved to be more than adequate for the needs of the area. It continued as a Congregationalist place of

worship with the Ebenezer as its parent until the mid 1950s. By then, there was a general decline in non conformism. Additionally, many of the congregation had moved away. For those who remained, the increasing motor traffic on Chatham Hill was becoming intolerable during worship.
The decision was made to sell the site. The remaining worshippers could use the Ebenezer. The money raised would go towards building a new church, the Emanuel Free Church, at Weeds Wood. The former Congregationalist Sunday School was eventually taken over by the Jehovah's Witnesses who renamed it the Kingdom Hall. The former Sunday School on Chatham Hill is still used for teaching purposes. Since the Jehovah's Witnesses left, it has become the Shi Kon Martial Arts Centre, teaching both adults and children the art of self defence.

As you can see this was perfect for us: we had a meeting with all of our club instructors who agreed to use the money raised from gradings, equipment and seminars to help pay for it. I took a business loan to buy it, put my house up for collateral, renovated it, put in new flooring, and started using it as an HQ and dojo in 1996, then most of the instructors left, taking their clubs with them. We sold our house and built a flat over the top to consolidate, either gave our own external clubs away or closed them and located ourselves fully at the dojo paying off the business loan just a few years later.

This is a short 'walk around the dojo' we wrote to describe its contents.

Let's start with the Shinto Buddhist shrine known as the 'kamidana'. It was presented to founder Steve Rowe by one of his Iaido instructors Vic Cook and is a replica of the shrine in the 'honbu' dojo in Japan dedicated to Fudo Miyoo, the guardian of martial arts dojos in Japan and also guardian of the Buddhist way. His statue is on the window sill facing and guarding the dojo doorway. He has a ferocious expression on his face to scare demons, is surrounded by flames for ferocity, stands on stone for immovability and holds a sword and weighted rope to cut away and bind evil. Inside the shrine is his picture along with a mirror and pearls which according to legend were used to tempt the sun goddess and founder of Japan, Amatarasu out of her cave. On the shrine is also salt, rice, alcohol and oranges to keep Fudo Miyoo nourished and happy along with flowers and a 'zen bow and arrow' to pierce illusion.

The photos either side of the shrine are of Steve's instructor in Wado Ryu Karate, Toru Takamizawa and his instructor Hironori Ohtsuka, the founder of the style.

In the corner is a golden statue of Bodhidharma presented to Steve by Shi Kon member Nathan Johnson, author of *Barefoot Zen* and *The Great Karate Myth* among many other titles. Bodhidharma brought Buddhism to China and the martial arts in the Shaolin Temple. This statue was rescued from a monastery in China by Nathan's family. The book in front of the statue is a healing book where we write the names of people to send healing to during our meditations.

Fudo Miyoo

The Tai Chi shrine has the ancient Tai Chi symbol as the centrepiece (often called the yin yang symbol), and represents the balance of the universe, the surrounding circle represents infinity along with the curved line down the middle (curved because it is spinning) and the black and white segments representing the opposing forces of the universe that the practice of Tai Chi will harmonise. The photos of the Yang family are Steve's lineage in Tai Chi in Hong Kong. The charts are of the body core and connected lines of power used in the martial arts. The 8 words on the sign in the middle are the principles of the Shi Kon training system and each one is a doorway to understanding an area of the arts that

Bodhidharma

put together mean that if all 8 are present whatever the student is doing will work. This is the heart of a principle based system.
The painting of the tiger was presented to Steve by some of his students as he was born in the Chinese 'year of the tiger' and it's one of the important animals in Kung fu.
The red and black logo on the rear wall is the Shi Kon 'mon' and was designed by Steve. It is a Buddhist 'dharma' wheel to represent the path to truth as taught by the Buddha and the 8 spokes are the path to that realisation and also the 8 directions we teach in our training system. Each spoke is leaf shaped to represent the story of when the Buddha was walking in the woods with one of his disciples who was worried that the Buddha would die not having taught everything that he knew. The Buddha picked up a handful of leaves and asked the disciple which was more, the leaves in the forest or the leaves in his hand, the disciple answered the leaves in the forest, to which the Buddha replied that all you need to understand is the leaves in his hand to understand all the leaves in the forest. This is analogous to his 4 noble truths and understanding the principles of the martial arts. The 4 circles represent the 4 Noble Truths of Buddhism and also the 4 distances we use in our martial arts training.
The 2 calligraphies either side of the logo were presented to Steve by his Japanese Iaido instructor Okimitsu Fuji: one is 'Shi Kon' that he drew when he named the association and means 'warrior spirit'

Steve Rowe

and the other one is 'hei jo shin' that he bought back from Japan; it was drawn by a zen priest and means 'keep your usual (highly trained) mind'.

The certificate on the back wall was presented to Steve by the government of the Czech Republic for his service in introducing and developing the martial arts in their country for over 30 years. The grading certificates in the foyer are of the senior instructors and the 9th Dan certificate was also awarded to Steve by the Czech government.

The doorstep with 'Shi Kon Budo Kan' written on it (meaning 'warrior spirit martial arts hall') is a gift from a student and there to remind students to clear their mind ready to learn as they bow when they enter the hall.

On the wall over the mirror is a picture of Steve presented to him by the first Tai Chi Coaching Programme and is flanked by two Japanese Temple Guardians photographed and presented to him by his friend Chris Rowen, a Goju 8th Dan, Shinto priest and former 'uchi deshi' (live in student) to Goju Kai founder Gyogen Yamaguchi. Further down is a painting of Kuan Yin, the Chinese goddess of mercy and compassion, an original painting given to us and painted by the talented Ray Hunt from Diablo Tattoo parlour and the person that did the tattoos on both Steve and Ann Rowe.

The two antique Chinese dragons on the window sill represent the wisdom of the martial arts as they are reptiles (bound to the earth) that can fly to heaven, usually by holding a magic pearl. There is a story connected to how Steve Rowe came across these that he may tell you if asked.

The engravings on the windows and the calligraphy on the middle wall are of the Buddhist heart sutra and focuses on the simplicity of an enlightened and intelligent heart. On the other window is the calligraphy for 'Budo' (Japanese for martial arts and 'to stop the spear').

The picture of the happy Chinese swordsman (representing Kui Xing, the chief star in the Big Dipper constellation) and butterflies were given to us by our students who founded Shi Kon Trinidad and it represents the lightness and happiness of martial arts training.

As we built the flat, my wife made protective symbols to put between the walls of both dojo and flat and wrote protective symbols on the underside of every roof tile as the builders put the roof on. The reason that I am documenting this is to show why it is important to build and develop strong roots in your arts, buildings and club. My lineages in all of the arts go directly back to their beginnings: in Karate they go directly back to the founder of Wado Ryu, in Iaido they go back to the founders in the 1675 and in Tai Chi directly to the Yang Family. Each lineage is represented in the dojo, it is mindfully maintained and when you enter you know you have walked into a traditional dojo with those strong roots both in the orient and in the community.

Developing a business and lifestyle, it is important to build these strong roots, firstly develop yourself, be as good as you can be in your chosen art or trade, learn properly from the best. The Japanese have a saying 'shu ha ri'. 'Shu' is to internalise a traditional system of learning until you become it; this is expected to take around 20 years of study with a master. 'Ha' is to be able adapt that learning to suit you without losing any of the essence. 'Ri' is to have fully internalised both stages until there is no system, because you are it, whatever you do will still embody the ideas and principles and you are free of all structures and technique.

My daughter Caroline runs the admin for the dojo. She is a black belt and has been a part of the club since she was a child for around 38 years. Her husband Mikey teaches all the classes, even my granddaughter is a black belt and trains. The 'family' atmosphere adding to the generations of lineage gives it a complete personal as well as martial lineage.

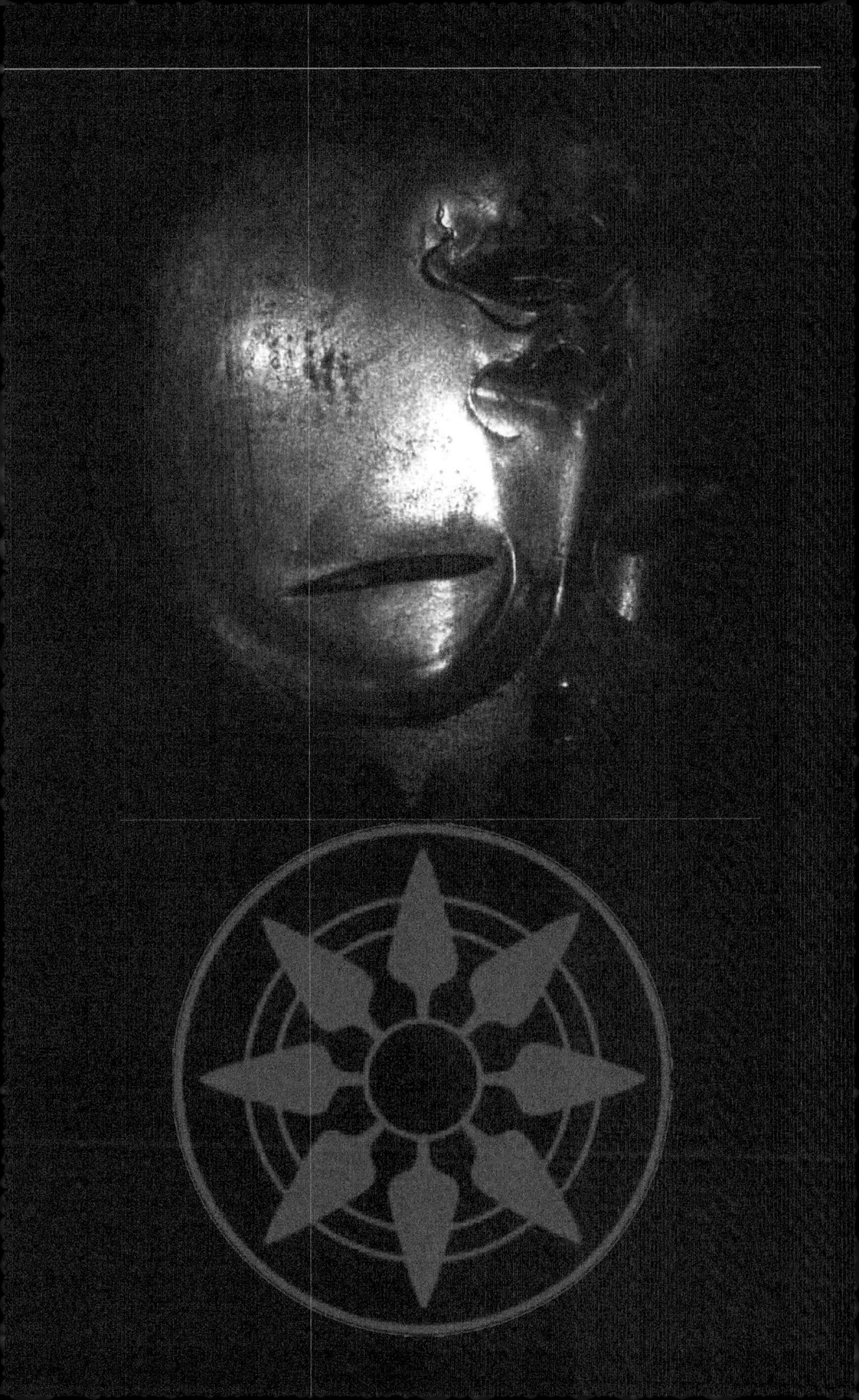

CHAPTER 10
The Business

Out of the Four Noble Truths that Buddha gave, we have already covered the first three of suffering, the cause of suffering and the cessation of suffering. The Fourth Truth of the Eightfold Path - which is depicted in the 'dharma wheel' that is our logo, a wheel with 8 spokes - is the perfect advice for living and how to conduct business. It breaks down into three parts that are wisdom, ethics and meditation.

The first two are right (middle way) perspective and resolve. To have that perspective broad enough to see and take everything in before applying objective and critical thinking and the measured resolve to see everything through. The second part is how to conduct yourself ethically with 'right' speech, behaviour and livelihood. Words can cause as much harm as weapons and can also create a lot of good with support and encouragement. Our behaviour is an obvious point and one that can create trust and loyalty. Right livelihood means to earn your living by causing no harm, and supporting your family and community. The final three are right effort, mindfulness and concentration, that we have already covered in this book. The Buddha said that it didn't matter what your religion or culture was, that if you lived to these eight points, you could not help but become enlightened. I would add that you will also build a positive business and community around you!

I see friends and other martial art school owners either going to shallow business gurus telling them how to fill their clubs by using their pro forma adverts and then how to maximise profits by raising prices, upselling expensive memberships and selling loads of additional equipment or tying students into costly contracts; or going to the more reputable ones who are only bastardising Buddhism with their own 'guru speak' and bending it to suit their business, yet all the original, teachings are contained within their traditional systems, their culture and are free and online!

The Shi Kon Tai Chi Coaching Programme

When I had my near death experience in 2015 and was in hospital for five months and everyone thought I was dying, I meditated for fifty-two days, wrote a poem each day on my phone and self published the book on Amazon from my phone. I thought that was going to be my legacy – and then I got better. When I was in hospital, my good friends and students kept the dojo going, travelling from Basingstoke, Essex and London to teach. One of them, Gavin King suggested that as I couldn't travel well, with chronic fatigue and a fused leg it might be a good idea to start a Coaching Programme. As it turned out it was a brilliant idea.

I put one together aiming for people from other martial arts to show them how Tai Chi could give them the 'missing piece' of the internal work and roots of their own arts. In 2018 I ran the first basic 10-month 'Monk style' programme, consisting of the neigong (internal work), qigong (energy work), the Yang Chen Fu form and basic push hands work. Then, at the students request, I followed it with a 20-month 'Warrior style' Advanced Programme, consisting of the Chong Chuan (Long Boxing), Dao (broadsword), Jian (double edge sword), Chiang (spear), all done both solo and in pairs, with applications and a lot of push hands drills. These have now been running for over six years and over 100 people qualified, many of whom opened their own Shi Kon Tai Chi clubs.

Despite my many health problems emanating from those knee replacements in 2007, the various challenges we have faced as a family (my wife and daughter also have health challenges), the strong roots we have, the trust and loyalty of family, friends and students have meant that to this day more, than 40 years later, we are still running a highly successful club and business that is investing in both our personal development and that of the community.

Martial Arts in the Media

There is a lot of misinformation spread by martial arts business gurus about the use of media to advertise their products, but let me give my history in it first.

I started writing books in the 80s. I wrote a self defence book that one of my Norwegian students published for me, then I was asked to 'ghost write' a book for the Red Power Ranger, Austin St John, and when the publishers realised how well I was known in the martial arts, they added my name as the author and asked me to also write the philosophical parts of the video. I then helped write and published two excellent books on Karate entitled *Concepts Of Karate* with Toru Takamizawa, under the publishing name of TAKRO (Takamizawa and Rowe). These can still be downloaded free on my blog. I wrote and self published a book on children's Karate with my Iaido Sensei Vic Cook, drawing the excellent cartoons. As I said earlier in the book, whilst in hospital, I wrote the book of poems entitled *Warrior's Mind* that is still available from Amazon.

It has taken me years to get around to writing this book. It was proposed to put together a book collating the best of my social media and blog posts, but I didn't feel that would be honest, as I needed to have a consistent thread running through my philosophy with the context of how it came about. I hope that I have done that here. Everything I write here about the martial arts, my dojo and coaching programmes can be applied to any other business.

Back in the 70s, when the magazines (the only source of media available) focused on the sporting aspect of Karate, I started writing for Combat magazine about the deeper and more traditional aspects. When Traditional Karate magazine came on the market in the 80s, they asked me to write several columns a month for them so I wrote 'Voice From The Deep', a column from my meditations, 'Coaching Corner', from the Instructor's point of view, 'Business File', about the business of martial arts and various other reporting, topics and interviews. In those days, photographs had to be done on film, so I had to take a roll of film for one article and hope there would be enough

Online magazines seemed the way forwards, but as we have become the nation of 'instant news' and access, a monthly magazine doesn't work. I also noticed that people didn't want to read anything more than a few paragraphs at a time and were looking on their devices every day, so we had to learn to be more concise and write in a more 'chatty' manner. As a result, I set up a blog, transferred around 300 articles that I'd written for the mags on to there and posted regularly. To date, I'd been writing for martial arts magazines for around 30 years; I tried to launch the online Martial Arts Guardian along with three others, but I really wasn't in synch with what they wanted to do. The time for magazines had come to an end; before the internet, they were without a doubt the best way to reach out to anyone interested in martial arts, but as everyone could get onto the internet on their phones, they all collapsed.

As I was at the heart of Karate politics, I took care of interviewing all the senior practitioners. When MAI started their awards ceremonies, I refused to sit on the panel or have anything to do with it because I didn't believe people should pay to get awards. I had nothing against them doing it, just didn't want to be a part of it but that was the end of our relationship. By this time I'd been writing for good quality photos, print the article and send it all by post in time for the publication date. A time consuming process... I didn't write to promote myself. My reason for doing it was to promote the Arts. To this day I don't know what I did to offend the editor but he stopped publishing my articles and I left. The magazine subsequently collapsed and the editor of MAI asked me to write for the up and coming Martial Arts Illustrated. I wrote the 'Beyond Technique' column, and 'Samurai On The Door' along with well known night club doorman Dennis Jones.

probably have 450 or so articles on there, and the good thing is that they remain online for permanent reference and are viewed worldwide.

I can remember people saying that if only the public could have access to information, they would be better educated. Then all the information in the world suddenly became accessible to them via their smartphone and they played games, watched porn and other salacious material. If anything, it is used to manipulate people, showing that the majority don't really change whatever access is available! Someone wrote that if a million monkeys were given typewriters, they'd eventually come up with the complete works of William Shakespeare. Boy, were they wrong! For those of us that like to research and communicate with other niche groups, though, it is a godsend.

For me, social media has been great. The ability to be able to reach people worldwide from my phone or iPad has saved me a fortune. I am also a concise writer, and to be able to write a philosophical message in just a few paragraphs, attach a picture from my phone and instantly post it to thousands of people has helped to keep me going and express myself on a regular basis. As my talent is to teach very experienced people in my field, I have also been able to easily reach out to this niche audience.

The secret to success in our area of social media is authenticity. If you have deep roots, if you have taken the time discover who you really are, develop your skills and personality, you can write from the heart. There is a saying that if you go to a library there are the original books written by inspired people, then there are books written by academics about the content of those books, then the books about those books and so on, branching out like a tree. You need to be able to get to the original works of inspired people and eventually become one of them. Good people will recognise if you are authentic, and this is an important point.

Recruiting

Many years ago a friend told me about a company that recruited people for gyms. He had used them for his dojo and had a lot of new clients. I foolishly agreed to use them, they created adverts, special reduced price packages and went down to the town and signed people up in the High Street. In 3 weeks they had recruited eighty-five people: I was amazed! Those eighty-five students literally disappeared in weeks. Most had been pressure sold the membership, were a very low calibre of character for martial arts training and some unable to tie their own shoe laces! Up until then our attrition rate of recruits was very low. It was one of the biggest mistakes I'd made, but I learned that as much as students choose us, it is important for us to choose them!

Many dojo work really hard on mass recruitment, but their attrition rate is horrendous. The other problem with that is if you are bringing in people that don't understand what they are in for, the bad people stay and the good leave. Doing seminars around the world I got to see many bad clubs where the instructor wasn't very good at coaching and ended up with students that weren't very good at training. The instructor often blamed the students! This is why I was saying that you are only as strong as your weakest point. You have to fully understand yourself and what and who you want to teach. You need to be skillful in what you do and how you teach it. You also have to create the right environment. Then your advertising needs to target the right people.

One of the problems we have in the martial arts is the companies that target the less successful: they get the pro forma website, the pro forma advertising, the easy to teach rotating curriculum and the only advancement the instructors get is 'networking' with the company's other instructors and how to collate the statistics for how much profit they're making. They end up recruiting mainly children, because they can get by with games and time wasting drills, and the children leave before there's any real expectation of skill. Therefore, the instructors only become business managers.

It's important to not get lumped in with these clubs and have to compete with them. We need to project out into the community who we are, what we do, how we do it and teach. Firstly, we get out into the community, we work with local charities to help and raise money for them. We include ourselves into local health promotions to prove the benefits of what we teach. We demonstrate what we do at local events.

Schools are a local resource: at one time, supported by the School Sports Community Programme, we ran twenty-five 'after schools clubs' that were all highly successful and did a lot of good in the community until the government withdrew funding for the programme. When you're a well recognised member of the community and operate a child safety programme recognised by them, schools are happy to distribute your leaflets in their school bags, include you in their newsletters and communications and let you do demonstrations at their assemblies.

Teaching my Annual Summer Course in Jizerka, Czech Republic, with Aikido Sensei Robert Mustard 8th Dan (right) and Joe Thambu 8th Dan (left)

The saying 'a good salesman only has to go out on the road once', is a good one. If he finds the right customers, sells them the right product, stays in touch with them, becomes a reliable supplier and friend and provides a good service, they will never need to go elsewhere and will recommend him to other clients.

This is the support we need whatever our business, behind anything we do on the internet and social media. If our potential students or customers already know of us from our local presence we are already in front of anyone else. Our website and social media pages, photos, posts and writings need to accurately reflect who we are, what we do and what they might already know about us. Our presence and information on Google must be accurate and up to date. Our website needs to have all the information people need on the front page and be easily navigable, so that people can get to information they need in one click. How many times have you come off a website because it is too hard to navigate, or you can't find the information you need? How many times have you given up because they don't have a clear pricing structure? Instructors often say that they don't get many students from their website and I can see why. Don't forget it is also the right kind of student that we want, not just a lot.

Posting on Facebook can be a nightmare, because it is not just about followers, friends and engagement, but the right kind of followers, friends and engagement. Our business and personal pages need to be separate unless we are selling ourselves as a person. We shouldn't post too much or too little: too much and the reader will 'unfollow', if we're spamming their feed, or we will drop off if we post too little. Photos and videos with text are important as are posts, reels and stories. Don't judge just by 'engagements', 'views' and 'visits' but by results. We need to write as authentically as possible and from our own direct knowledge: the better prospects will see through 'copy and paste' posts from elsewhere, standard motivational memes and photographs copied from elsewhere.

Learn to take good photographs, it is not so hard these days with the high definition cameras on smartphones. Get permission from students, parents and carers before we photograph anyone, so that the words are ours and the photos and videos are about what really goes on at the club or business. Make sure to get genuine testimonials from students or customers and don't forget to put them on Google, websites and social media. Encourage students and customers to share posts to get a natural spread of information. We haven't done any paid advertising for years, but if we do, we thoroughly research and choose to whom and where they are directed.

Personally, I found Facebook good, Instagram okay, Twitter mainly politics and TikTok is for needy people craving attention, but that is just a personal view, you have to research for yourselves. Most of our students in the dojo come from personal recommendations, Google and our website, with some from social media. My coaching programme comes mainly from personal recommendation and/or Facebook.

Synergy

There is a synergy to be found: when we have found that portal to the infinite, we can put who and what we are into perspective, we become authentic, then we are the same in our personal and professional life. We don't have to wear different masks for each part and others consciously and subconsciously can see that and they will be instinctively drawn to you. You will keep the good people and the bad will naturally shy away from you, because they will know that you can see through them.

Success is different for each of us, but when we find that meaning and purpose and make a positive contribution to our society, community and those closest to us, this can define our success. As teachers we then find that our teachings will naturally reflect not only in the martial skill and technique of the student, but in their lifestyle and business as well.

Robert Musil

One of my students, Robert Musil, the son of the founder of Shi Kon in the Czech Republic, explains this really well in a testimonial:

> I was unlucky enough to be born in early eighties behind the Iron Curtain in what is now the Czech Republic. On the other hand, I was lucky enough to live through the fall of the Iron Curtain and through the ever so happy nineties, which brought peace and hope to Europe. For me personally, the fall of the Iron Curtain brought one more thing in 1990 and that was Steve Rowe. Steve (as I know him), was invited by my Father to teach the free and democratic Police Self Defence Instructors, including some of our special services and Presidential Bodyguards of Mr. Václav Havel (famous Czech President and Dalai Lama's personal friend) and has done so for many years.
>
> In the meantime he has become a huge influence in the martial arts in the Czech Republic. He is seen regularly on our sporting TV station, and in 2017 he was awarded 9th Dan by our Martial Arts Governing body for the support and knowledge he has

Steve Rowe

Me (centre) with Robert Musil (right) and his sister
Tereza (left) our Tai Chi Coach in the Czech Republic

given us. His annual Summer School in Jizerka is a very popular event and runs for more than 30 years.

Steve has always been willing to offer his vast knowledge of martial arts and philosophy to us with a Buddhist spirit – and at that time this quality actually brought something unique to our country. It was given to us free of charge and free of any limits. He has introduced us to several martial arts under the Shi Kon International banner, namely Wado-Ryu Karate, Aikido, Iaido, Jodo and Shi Kon 'Yang Style' Tai Chi Chuan.

During my years of training with Steve (thirty three by now), I have grown old, made it through schools of all sorts, gained several World and European WKC Karate titles in kata, started my legal services carrier and become managing equity partner of a Czech legal subsidiary to the Europe wide consultant company VGD, member of London based CLA Global, ranking as the third largest in Czech Republic for M&A among such as KPMG, PwC, Deloitte or EY.

I trained in Karate with him from when I was a small child and took up Shi Kon Tai Chi when I was 15 years old. Through continuous in-depth-training I have learned not only the external skills but also internal skills such as mindfulness, focus and the 'soft cotton boxing' strategies. I use them not only in my training but in my entire life. Some of my friends, top ranked managers and business owners practice Shi Kon Tai Chi with me and can easily testify to the positive impact it has on their everyday life and business.

Steve's analytical approach to martial arts and his life philosophy has brought many benefits to our club, association and everyday life here in Czechia. It has helped all of us on what was a very hard journey from a nearly underground Karate club in the communist years in a country tested by national socialism, communism and soviet invasion, to one of the most outstanding and world wide recognised clubs in a free and prosperous society.

I strongly recommend Steve's Shi Kon Tai Chi Coaching Programme to every martial arts coach who is serious about their study and teaching. I would also very strongly recommend it to every professional person who is serious about their personal development and looking to gain a competitive edge to their craft and more abundance and mindfulness in their practice.

Also, I would like to contribute a personal bit. I am a huge fan of early mornings and as such I do start my morning at 5AM everyday with my Tai Chi exercise. It has really helped me to manage the huge stress levels that are connected with my line of business. If you are a fan of early mornings or any other morning routine, I can only recommend adding Shi Kon Tai Chi to it."

You can clearly see how it has permeated every part of his life and contributed to his success.

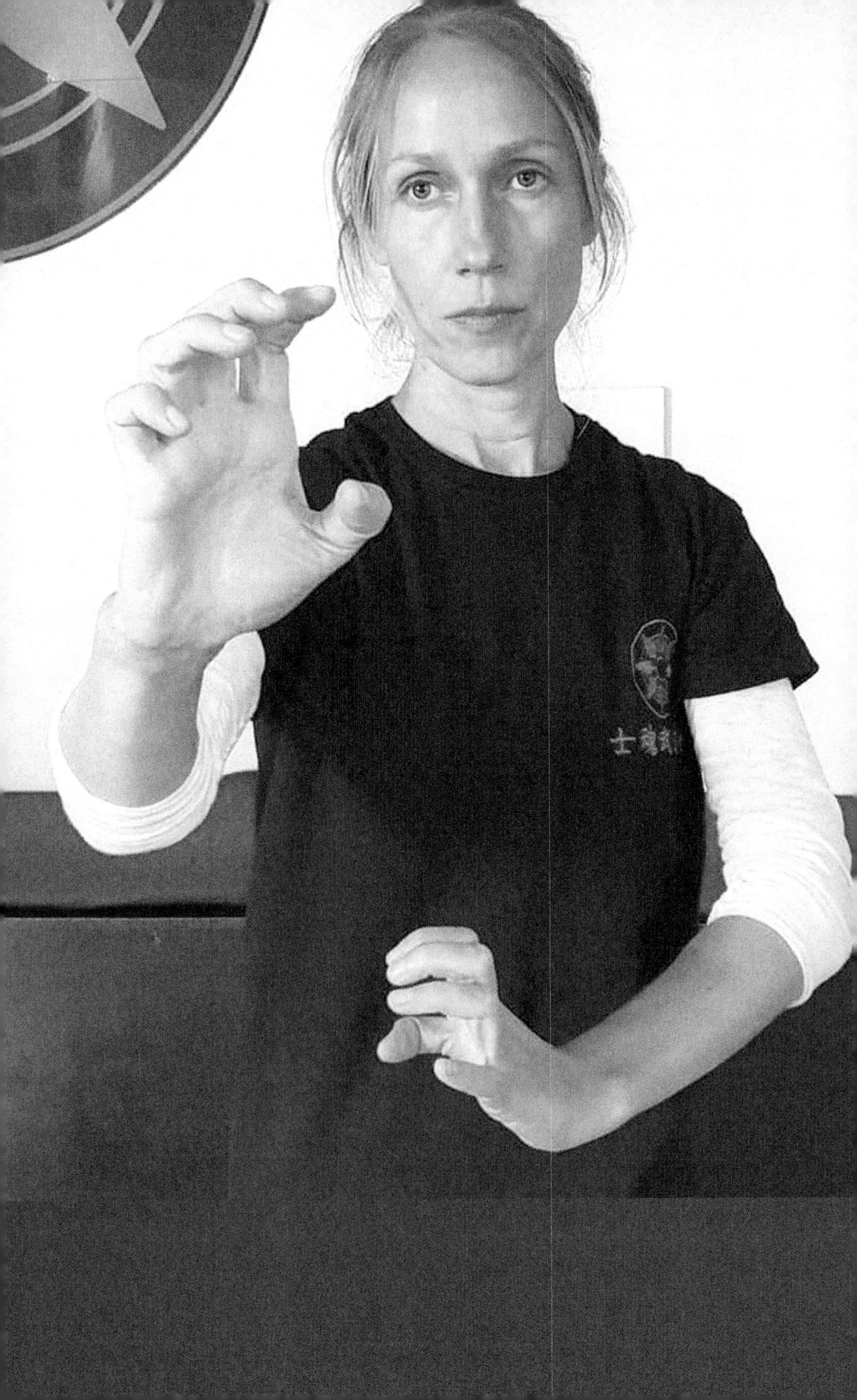

CHAPTER 11
Students and Teaching

We often talk about what makes a good instructor and what makes a good club, but what happens when we turn that on its head and ask what makes a good student? The one thing that I discovered was that if I knew how to be a good student, I could get far more out of my instructors than anybody else, and that as an instructor I am far more inclined to teach a good student thoroughly than a bad one.

The inescapable fact is that many instructors don't get to choose their students. Sometimes they teach with the idea that it is wrong to favour students and therefore 'stick it out' with what they consider a bad one, and sometimes the reasons are financial. Either way, however, I quickly discovered that there are ways to get far more than anyone else was getting and I didn't have to compromise my morals to achieve it! This is the advice I give to those that really want to progress in their training:

> You don't have to like a person to teach them well, a student doesn't have to like an instructor to learn from them: all it takes is a bit of patience and tolerance on both sides to get there. I've had a love/hate relationship with many students in the past and I can understand that they hate me for being blunt with them and for making them do things that they didn't want to. If you don't push them beyond what they think are their limits, how are they going to improve? If they don't have that basic faith and trust in me even if they don't like me, or what I'm making them do, they can never grow as a martial artist. I never worried about popularity, just results.

What can a student do to make the relationship work better? This is the magic formula that I used to get that extra tuition and information that the others never got.

Always pay your fees. It seems obvious but it isn't to many. Never barter on a price. Always pay for your lesson whether you turn up or not. If you want that regular spot, book it with money, then it's always yours and a bond of trust is formed. There is nothing worse than a student that books an instructors time, cancels and doesn't pay. If someone who does pay regularly comes along they will naturally give the time to them and you will forfeit yours. The instructor will also not be inclined to teach an irregular person well because they will see them as untrustworthy and think that they are wasting their time. If you are a long term student, raise the fees yourself, as it is unlikely that the instructor will do it, and when you show that you value their time and consider their well being, it will be appreciated.

Always make notes. Learn a training shorthand of matchstick men, arrows and keywords so that when you get home you will remember what you have been taught. Ask the instructor to film you doing what you have just learned on your phone, and if you are lucky he will give advice whilst doing it. If he doesn't want to do this get someone else to do it as soon as possible afterwards. Between lessons train continuously on what you have been taught and think about it all of the time. Every time a question arises, write it down to ask on your next lesson. There is nothing more encouraging for an instructor than a student who pays attention, makes notes, trains hard between lessons and then asks questions on the next lesson.

Listen and pay attention to what you are being taught. Don't give your opinion. Don't talk about what you have done or what you think, because you're paying the instructor to give you the benefit of their experience. There is nothing more boring than a student who pays the instructor so they can talk to them for a couple of hours about what they think and have done. Every minute is important, and not just from a financial point of view: that instructor could be dead tomorrow and you're wasting precious time with your own ego. If you are asked: "What do you want to do?", remember that the Instructor is being polite. Answer: "Whatever you think I need to work on". You are likely being taught a system and it is best to learn it in the right sequence put together by the expert, not randomly by your own desires.

Develop respect and care. If the instructor is doing their best for you and you are for them, mutual respect is earned naturally. If there is anything you can do to help or support them in their home life, club and association development, do it, because it means that your teaching environment is less likely to be affected by outside influences and it is good to care. I have represented my instructors on Governing Body Committees, helped them to write books, shoot videos, buy houses, helped with legal problems, opened clubs for them, taught on their seminars and helped them bring over their instructors to the UK.

Every time you reach a milestone in your training, like a grading, winning a tournament or opening your own club, always thank your instructor before doing anything else and always give them credit for what they have taught you. Nowadays that courtesy has all but disappeared and you can see students prancing around with their new grade or trophy and everyone patting them on their back whilst the instructor sits quietly in the corner. It is not inappropriate to buy them a small thank you gift or at least offer a thank you before celebrating yourself.

It is easy to teach just the surface of a system and the student would never know. Often that is done as a test to see if they are worthy or capable of receiving deeper instruction. Courtesy is a given, respect is earned both ways. When the student and instructors chi is 'in agreement', respect has been earned and they are capable of working through the hard times together; then the 'hidden levels' can be taught. Nothing is being held back, it is just that the environment has to be right. The surface teaching is known as 'eating sweet', and the deeper levels as 'eating bitter'. 'Eating sweet' is full of flashy moves and certificates and 'eating bitter' is made of sweat, blood, pain and a system that gradually alters body and mind.

By all means, find the right club and instructor, but remember that they are also looking for the right student.

The Plus and Minus Zones

This is a great technique to increase mindfulness. I draw a line in my mind and call it the 'zero' line. All the time that I am in a mindful state I'm above the line and in the 'plus' zone, all time that I am not mindful, I am in the 'minus' zone. At the end of the day I count the hours that I was in the plus and minus zones, and if I spent more time in the 'plus' zone I feel that I have moved forwards.

I get the students to do this while they practice as well. They have to focus to remember the skills and sequence of a form, but once internalised they can get really lazy. It is a bit like driving to a place that you go to each day; when you can remember the way, you often arrive not remembering the journey, as you did it on autopilot. It is a good exercise to not do that and focus on improving your driving and awareness skills. The basic Tai Chi form takes around 20 minutes. Once learned, it is too easy to go on autopilot rather than go deeper and increase your skill level. I noticed that most people find it really hard to pay attention for any longer than a few minutes and either slip into a lethargy or are distracted.

The same thing happens in meditation: when your mindfulness does slip away, you don't notice it and when you realise what has happened you have to dispassionately reinstate it. The more you do this, the better your control of concentration and awareness gets.

Teaching Children

I remember that on a coaching course I attended the teacher said that we had to remember that children were not 'mini adults'. That of course is true, but I remember thinking that adults are 'big children', so everything I write below about children we can also apply to adults with very little variation.

It is important that children enjoy their training. Instructors have to be careful to not become anything more than childminders in a martial arts suit. Children need to be taught how to pay attention, how to learn and how not be too easily distracted. The advantage that an instructor has is that the children want to be there as opposed to school where they have no choice.

We have an important role to play in a child's life, we need to not only teach them how to pay attention and learn, but also how to stay healthy, how to socialise with other children and how not to be bullied and abused by both other children and adults.

Teaching children to meditate

Children have to be taught in a different way to adults: it should be threaded through their normal training. To ask them to just sit or stand still without proper instruction will make them uncomfortable and not want to do it. Mindfulness is taught through posture and breath to induce calm, and included in all slower technical learning by also getting them to focus on one aspect of the movement. This way it becomes a normal aspect of their training.

Children can sit or lay down in a good posture and breathe naturally but a bit more deeply, and focus on doing their techniques and forms perfectly. To ensure their minds don't wander, I usually get them to raise their hand when they finish. This is also good technical training used by top athletes.

Mindfulness is learning to pay attention, so children should never be 'let off the hook' in class. They should always pay attention to the coach and always be positioned in attention or ready stance, at ease, seated with arms and legs folded, or in a martial position. Instruction should be given by varying techniques and positions, stimulating them to pay attention in order to know what to do. Single repetition allows their mind to be lazy and get distracted.

Eventually, when they have these skills, adult seated and standing postures can be practised and will not put them off by making it seem like a punishment.

In Karate we have a 'Dojo Kun', and each session we recite the primary rules. We designed a simple one for children that includes only four rules that the children recite each session - however, to be honest, they can also be applied to adults.

- Practice every day (an essential habit).
- Never attack anyone (a martial artist is to act as a peacemaker, not as a bully).
- Balance training, nutrition and rest (develop a healthy lifestyle).
- Have a good behaviour at all times (to make sure that they exercise discipline in their behaviour wherever they are).

These four rules help to develop good values. We also need to help them progress in life by learning how to have the right value in society. Following on from the 'metta' meditation, learning to respect oneself, respect others and value the environment, this is why we work with local groups and charities. To seek knowledge, not only in the martial arts and philosophy but to increase the appreciation of life and society, helping to achieve personal potential and contribute positively to the community.

Furthermore, we teach them to develop good manners: to always remember to say hello and goodbye, please and thank you and excuse me. To be on time, wait for their turn, sit and stand properly, ask before using, ask before moving, to not interrupt or yell out, swear or embarrass others. To show good behaviour by being responsible for their actions, to acknowledge that everyone has rights and responsibilities and that there are consequences for negative behaviour. That is showing care, courtesy and respect. Understanding that bullying and harassment aren't fair and hurt people and that rules are there to protect people's rights.

Good social skills develop self esteem, good values and good manners. People skills mean that they can communicate effectively with others, build and maintain friendships, work cooperatively in groups and teams, build and maintain friendship, manage and resolve conflict, make good choices in challenging situations and avoid antisocial behaviour.

Developing people skills means to maintain a happy demeanour, use good manners, acknowledge others, greet others by using their name, look at them when talking, listen to them, accept your differences, respect their opinions and compliment them when warranted.

We make sure to focus on controlling personal space, how to deal with bullies and unwanted advances from adults. This is what I consider an important poem that I wrote on bullying:

>Bullying is not always obvious,
>Sometimes it's physical abuse,
>Sometimes it's verbal and persuasive,
>And sometimes it's on the screen you use.
>The punching and kicking is obvious,
>The name calling, taunting and rumour,
>Destroying someone's reputation can be more hidden,
>Done by nasty gossip and humour.
>Recruiting others makes it seem legitimate,
>Peer pressure makes it seem right,
>When many agree to make one suffer,
>Surely that makes it alright?
>Bullies often have high social standing,
>This empowers them with the crowd,
>They are quick to be aggressive,
>And the majority are scared to speak out.
>The victim will be lonely and nervous,
>And never seems to fit in,
>The emotional damage is permanent,
>And goes very deep within.
>The bully will suffer the same,
>But have learned to hide it well,
>Be manipulative nasty and narcissistic,
>And really as dark as hell.
>To make sure we don't bully or assist,
>We have to be emotionally secure,
>Be ready to stand up for the bullied,
>And not give in to our fear....

It is important to keep records of bullying, including a diary and photographs of any injuries; record conversations where possible. Some schools don't want to admit to the problem of bullying, so they will try to pass it off as 'six of one and half a dozen of the other'. Don't accept this and be prepared to go to the head teacher, school board and eventually your MP.

Advice to Parents on Training and Grading

Children just love to train. Most normal children will accept grades and rewards as and when they arrive and are not too concerned by them, their love is to be a part of a club, move their bodies and learn.

Wise parents give them the gift of putting them into a good club and letting them experience that unhindered. Damaged parents push their children to fulfil their own ambitions vicariously and pass that damage onto their children. A good instructor will only grade when the child is ready, irrespective of a pushy parent. This puts pressure on to the child, ultimately making them feel that they are a disappointment and they inevitably give up, feeling that they are a failure.

So here are a few dos and donts:
- Don't tell a child that they are ready for grading, leave that to the instructor.
- Don't compare your child to others in the club, they all progress at different rates.
- Don't coach your child from the sidelines, that makes you really 'pushy'.
- Don't 'push' an instructor to grade your child as that will only upset them and your child.
- Do ask for feedback on what your child can do to improve their training (good instructors love that).
- Do encourage your child to train and enjoy their training as much as possible.
- Do train yourself so that you can understand the process. Parents and children that train together at home bond and do extremely well.
- Do watch your child training to show interest.
- Do congratulate them for taking part, whether they pass or fail.

Gradings will then come in their own time and when they are ready.

We all love our children, but it is easy to damage them without realising it and make them feel like they are a failure. Children progress at different rates at different ages. It also depends on natural ability, on what else is going on in their life and on what kind of support you give them.

Who would want their child wearing a grade that they weren't worth? That has to be the worse thing a pushy parent and weak instructor could ever do to a child.

Guidance to Adults

This leads me quite nicely to some guidance that I put together to for my adult friends and students, borne out of my own experience.

- Don't make friends easily. In this age of 'Facebook friends' and 'networking' friends, it is too easy to mix up the difference between 'acquaintances' and people that you know, to what a friend actually is. Friendship is formed over time, behaviour and events. These are the people that you know you can trust, because you have both proven it time and time again. If you make just a handful of real friends in a lifetime, you are a lucky person.

- Always work on your mind and perspective 24/7. I have talked about this quite a bit in this book, but we do need to constantly remind ourselves right through each day, because it is too easy to fall back into bad habits.
- Always pay your way and live within your means. Reliability, honour and trustworthiness with money is really important. If you think that someone has forgotten that you owe them money, trust me, they haven't. They are just being nice about it: they are too embarrassed to keep reminding you and will definitely have your card marked.
- If you help somebody, do it because it is right, not to make them indebted to you. Otherwise, you have only done it to accrue a favour. There is a lot of merit in helping people and then forgetting about it. Believe me they won't.
- People you have helped will often stab you in the back, but don't let it become your problem. I hear so many people say: "That's it, I'm not helping anyone ever again." That is a shame, because you have then allowed that person to affect you negatively and spoil your good character.
- People you have taught will often never give you credit – mostly that is a good thing, because that kind of student rarely gets it right. Once taught, you can't take it back. My experience is that people that don't give you credit for your teaching have never understood it properly, so it is a good thing. I give a lot of information out for free on my blog and on social media, because I feel it is my duty to promote good philosophy and quality martial arts.
- Judge everyone by their actions not their words. It is too easy to be taken in by what people say. However, pay attention to what they do and listen to your instincts: that is the most reliable guide.
- Always get money out of the way first, thus everybody clearly understands and there is no confusion. Con men rely on you being embarrassed to talk about money. Always be up front with what you are charging and don't be afraid to make others be clear about it, as it saves a lot of bad feeling. Never trust anyone that is vague about money.
- There are so many people with so much enthusiasm and the inability to see it through. When people start with a really high level of enthusiasm they often burn out fast. It is easy to support

them and get caught up, to suddenly find that your investment fades away just as fast.
- Never be distracted by shiny objects. A common mistake with teachers is that some attractive students can appear to be committed and have talent and will occupy all their teaching time and effort to give up really quickly, while the quiet student working away in the background is the person most likely to make it all the way through. Never let anyone occupy your time with a lot of talk and not enough action.
- Never drop you standards for anyone – ever. A golden rule. The amount of times I have had parents trying to 'persuade' me to grade their child that was not ready, instructors asking me to grade their students that were not ready, one wealthy one even wanting to buy me a dojo to grade him, even though he wasn't good enough, so that he could qualify as a referee and double grade three of his students allowing them to compete in team kata! I obviously wouldn't do that and he thankfully went elsewhere. I have also had instructors ask me to grade a brown belt to black, even though they would clearly never make the standard, because they were a good secretary to the club… but should I give all of the above a belt they were not good enough to wear - and they knew it - and likely be the laughing stock of the other students?
- Always read the small print. I learned this the hard way and it was very expensive. If needs be, take the document away and read it thoroughly: these are days of small print and we tend to just accept documents and online small print without reading, this can lead to big mistake.
- If you want to do it right – don't do it wrong. This seems obvious, but everyone wants to learn in a hurry and think that if they expend a lot of effort, it will replace skill. You have to pay attention and work at a speed that means you can do it right, however slow you have to begin.
- Always light a room up when you enter and not when you leave. We all know people that we are always happy to see and those that we are glad when they leave. When reviewing your own demeanour, make sure that you are the first. I can never work out why people can't see when they are the latter, but I guess they are just self obsessed and can't see how others see them.

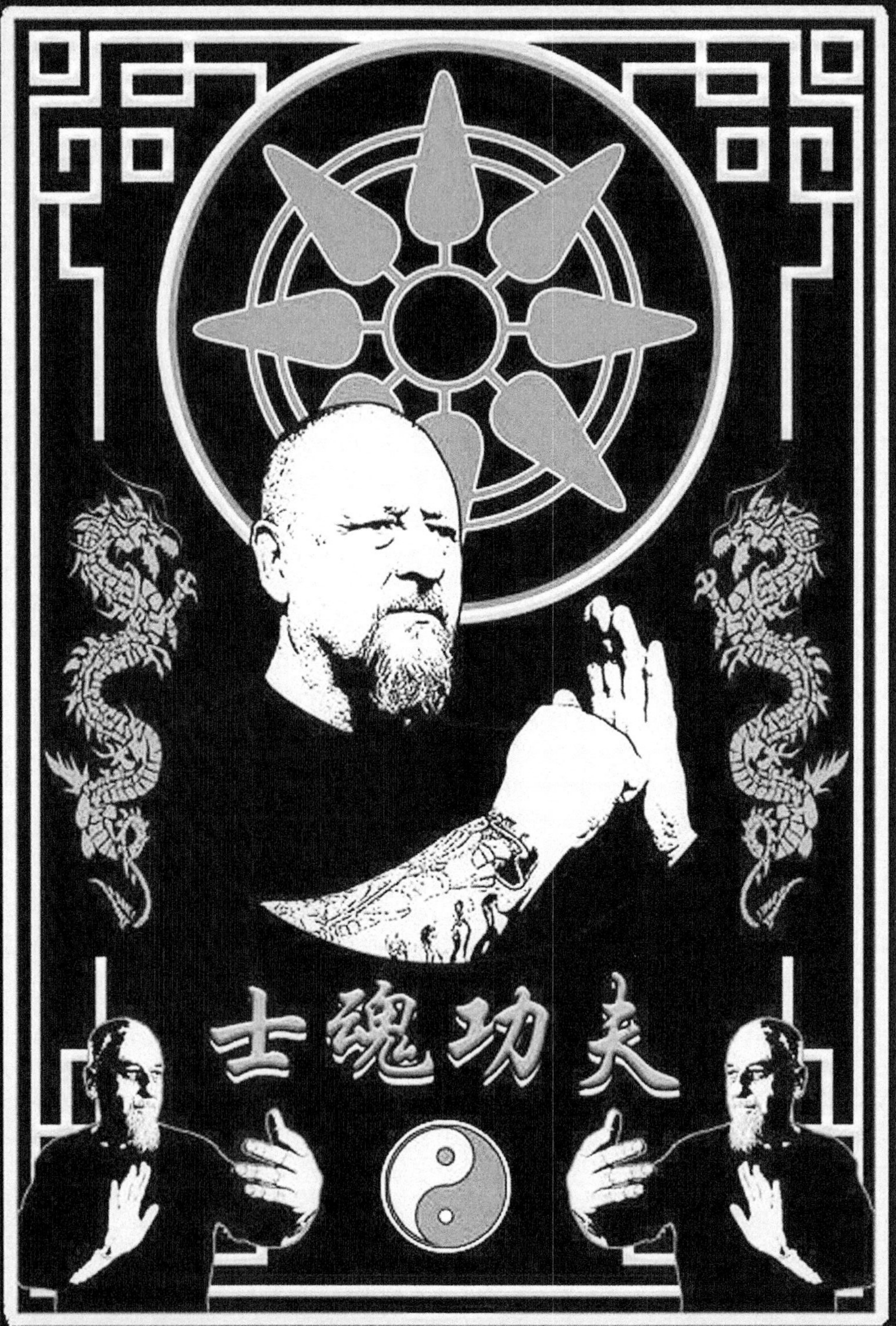
士魂功夫

CHAPTER 12
The Future

I feel that I have had a great life, discovering who and what I am through the practice of martial arts and mindfulness, learning to overcome the many challenges that I faced, forging deep roots in the community, developing my dojo and training systems, deep relationships with students, family and friends. My life has had fulfilment through both meaning and purpose, supporting family, friends and community, helping by being able to dispense the insight and wisdom gained from facing up to these various battles in health, training and business.

I have travelled widely training and teaching, developing my systems along the way, but what about the future? For me travelling is now limited, but luckily my students are happy to come to me. I only teach my Tai Chi Coaching Programmes but that is enough for me.

In the 50 years I have studied the martial arts and mindfulness, there have been many changes. There are millions more people training worldwide and the martial arts are a broad church. At the higher level there are some incredible athletes and knowledgeable people and at the bottom end there is a far wider spectrum of people with good intentions and low skill, and unfortunately more people out to empty your pockets and give nothing in return. The range goes from street fighter, to athlete, to Buddhist monk, so it's *caveat emptor* for the customer: very important to work out what you want from the arts and then do your due diligence, to make sure that wherever you go and who you take on to be your mentor is going to provide what you want.

Students have needs that drive them to train in the martial arts, and these tend to be media driven: from the need to get fit, lose weight, defend themselves; or they are excited by something they have seen in the movies. They will also be dictated by location and normally they will tend to find the nearest club. The chances of them finding the right club are minimal, it is only natural that they will probably change as they progress.

If you wanted to learn to swim, you'd go to the local pool and get a low level coach to learn the basics. As you improved, you might want to compete at regional level and go to a regional coach, then maybe you would want to progress to national level and go to a national coach, then perhaps at Olympic level so you would go to an Olympic coach. The same applies to martial arts. The requirements you had when you started will probably change as you progress, and you are quite likely to outgrow your local club and need to travel to find the right mentor.

The problems we have in the martial arts are the lack of governance, lack of standards and lack a designed pathway to excellence. The student has to find their own route through a minefield of misrepresentation in both competition and traditional standards. Most advertising seems to come from purely 'business' based clubs and is 'copy and paste' and 'pro forma' advertising from Martial Art business gurus and doesn't actually represent what is being taught.

Many instructors also get caught in this trap: they start with a love of their art and want 'spread the word' and have high standards, but unfortunately, in this day and age, expenses are high; they go to these business gurus and get trapped in a web of what they think is the 'quick fix', and end up teaching low level children's classes, as they are the easiest business option, and they hate it. I know so many of these people that are trapped. This is one of the reasons that I have written this book, to show that there is a different way.

Once I realised that my needs were far deeper than violence, and I recognised them from the Shaolin Temple in the TV programme *Kung Fu*, I followed my instincts and was prepared to do whatever it took on my journey of self discovery. I consider myself very lucky to have found all the right people at the right times, and I put that down to instinct and mindset, recognising when the doors of opportunity were opening to me. I have always put my own development first, because I knew that the results were permanent. If you're the best, you don't have to follow the fashions trends and people that want to go deeper will always come to you.

We have waiting lists for all our classes at the dojo, because people recognise that our roots go deep and most students come through recommendation. My coaching courses are fully booked with people travelling from all over the UK. They are usually experienced people that want that deeper elite teaching.

I don't think that we will ever have structure and governance in the martial arts: they can't agree on anything and Sport England gave up on Karate and many other arts. I set up MASA (The Martial Arts Standards Agency), a company limited by guarantee (non-profit making) with a basic set of standards, to show that you could put all the martial arts into one governing body regulating standards for advertising, business, safety, coaching and technical standards in each art. It was run by volunteers that were experts in their field with top accountants, lawyers and coaching experts giving their time and expertise on a voluntary basis. The government and Sport England turned a blind eye and it didn't get the support it needed, but it was worth a try.

Social media is awash with 'reels' and 'stories' with endless 'an idiot's guide to' basic techniques and as ever, the empty vessels make the most noise. I don't go on any martial arts pages, particularly Tai Chi, because they are filled with the same few people regurgitating the same endless childish arguments. This is why I write and post, because I feel that it is up to the more experienced 'old timers' to talk about the results of our studies. It is up to us to get our voices heard, not by joining in with the others (remember my analogy of wrestling with a pig), because on social media everyone has an equal voice; we don't want to argue or ridicule, but we need to speak of our findings and point to what is good and share it.

I feel that there is a lot of space for us to evolve, to become mature enough to get together and share without arguing, I spend a lot of time showing Martial Art teachers what we have in common: on my programmes currently I have instructors from different styles of Karate, Kung Fu, Krav Maga, Escrima, Ju Jitsu, MMA and Kickboxing. If you were watching a class, you wouldn't know who was who: this way we can respect each other. You don't grow by competing and denigrating each other, you grow by joining together, showing the benefits of what we teach and growing the market place. This is our currently unrecognised super power.

I talk about a compassionate lifestyle, about meditation, martial arts, politics, veganism and saving humanity. I'm often asked why I bother, since one person can't change the world. My answer is that we have to try. I know that I have influenced the lifestyle of thousands who have gone on to influence the lifestyles of thousands more. A compassionate change will not come from the top down, but from the bottom up. The more we talk and influence each other, the more politicians will arise to fulfil that need, that's the way the world works. Probably not in my lifetime, but we need to plant the seeds of the trees that future generations will sit in the shade of.

We are not born into this world, we are born out of it: we have always been here in one way or the other. Remember the quote, 'the shape changes but not the form'? Remember that our DNA takes us back to the beginning of time. We are immortal, we form the generations and environment of the future. We have this planet on a fully repairing lease, this is the true meaning of 'karma', action and reaction It is not about human laws and justice, but universal law and repercussion. This is what we need to be talking about and not just in quasi religious and political terms. We need to be discussing this in plain language with an understanding of what the repercussions are. If we leave anyone behind, it will come back to bite us on the bum.

Do I feel positive about the future? No. To be honest, I don't know. Humans should be mini gods, we have the power of a reflective conscious mind, we have the power to harmonise this world and live in a far more compassionate and harmonious relationship with each other and our environment. At the moment we are the plague, the pandemic, but we do have the power. One day it might dawn on us that we are not 'saving the planet', we are trying to save humanity.

The planet will allow us to survive to a point and then wipe us out and start again.

Remember, "Heaven and Earth are like a bellows, the shape changes but not the form, the more it moves, the more it yields". That is karma. It is up to us to recognise the full value of every human being, every animal and every part of our environment. Then we need to develop training, education and politics based on compassion. Compassion needs a soft front and a strong back. It can't be based on weakness or pity, it is a pure act that will balance our lifestyle, training, education, politics and the way we treat everyone and everything with respect.

Remember the Eightfold Path: right perspective, resolve, speech, behaviour, livelihood, effort, mindfulness and concentration. Done properly, that will develop a compassionate lifestyle, where we cause no unnecessary harm to others, have the right attitude, thought, action and reflection, and correct whatever we have done wrong. This quest for perfection, the continuous mental engagement without laziness and distraction, those will drive us in the right direction.

Perfection is not of this world. All the time we are driving this meat vehicle we are presented with challenges, that's the point. It is not the destination, it is the journey. We can slow everything down, we can smell the roses, we can enjoy the journey. We don't need to pick up that second arrow and stab ourselves with it; we don't need to pick at a scab, we can enjoy the healing, we can allow everything to happen at its natural pace. The result is a far more harmonious and successful lifestyle without any additional suffering.

It only takes one butterfly to flap its wings in the Amazon, one Rosa Parks to sit in the wrong seat on a bus, one speech by Martin Luther King, to start a chain of events that can change the world. Understand how karma works, never underestimate the power of small acts of kindness, passing them on, or an act of humanity or compassion. It may not be us in our lifetime, or the person we pass it onto, or the next generation, or the next, but everything counts and plays it's part.

I wrote this book because it was in me, it was instinctual, something inside that wanted to come out. Normally, it is just a blog or social media post, but this is more. I needed to give context from my life to show how a challenging existence can produce great results. I also needed to thread all of this together in one document to show how inspiration and insight can arise from almost everything you do in life and whatever happens, if you have the right mindset. We are always being encouraged to go out and conquer the world; whereas, it is equally not what you do, but also what you don't do that counts. It is not going out to to good, but equally causing no harm that is important. Quite often we don't need to go out to do something in life as we might miss all those doors that are open when life comes to us.

As my body gradually expires, now I don't have a 'bucket list'. I'm not desperate to see and do anything, I have a deeper happiness that is born from understanding that the only purpose of being alive is to just be alive. That is all nature intends, everything else is just human shit. To understand that I am not going anywhere even when my body has gone. There is no desperation from the indoctrinated 'self' to be something or be someone more than I am, I have no mask to wear. Sometimes we forget the that 'human being' is in fact 'being human'. I have been human for long enough.

Life has both light and darkness, the dark also sits behind everything, it's always there when the lights go out. People are often scared of the dark, but to be honest it is the 'self' that is afraid: the dark is the feminine, the mother, the healer, it is there for when we sleep, meditate and die. We yield to the dark and if it wasn't there, the light couldn't exist. Life can't exist without death, awake can't exist without sleep, male can't exist without female, happiness can't exist without sadness, health can't exist without illness. This is what this book is all about, the philosophy underlying all Asian culture, the yin and yang of our universe, why we have to have the soft front and the strong back.

At the moment, the balance in humanity is too yang, too masculine, requiring a far too combative attitude, because it lacks compassion, empathy and the ability to care for those that the attitude leaves behind. Therefore we have wars, killing, suffering, refugees, poverty, hunger and unnecessary sickness and suffering, along with an incredible amount of damage to our environment. If we don't balance this, it will be balanced for us.

We need to understand how to see our world and understand this balance: to do this we have to understand that we are the microcosm to the macrocosm. If we understand and learn how to balance ourselves then we will be able to naturally balance our environment. In Wiccan terms:

> As above, so below, if it harms none, let thy will be done.

To do this we need to develop a soft front and a strong back.

Thank you.

The Ran Network
https://therannetwork.com

Printed in Great Britain
by Amazon